9/22

There Are No
Accidents

Fr. Benedict J. Groeschel, C.F.R.
with John Bishop

There Are No Accidents

In All Things Trust in God

Our Sunday Visitor Publishing Division
Our Sunday Visitor, Inc.
Huntington, Indiana 46750

Copyright © 2004 by Our Sunday Visitor Publishing Division, Our Sunday Visitor, Inc. Published 2004
09 08 07 06 05 04   2 3 4 5 6

Our Sunday Visitor Publishing Division
Our Sunday Visitor, Inc.
200 Noll Plaza
Huntington, IN 46750

ISBN: 1-59276-120-8 (Inventory No. T172)
LCCN: 2004105634

Cover design by Monica Haneline
Interior design by Sherri L. Hoffman

Cover photos courtesy of:
Grassroots Renewal Project
119 Eagle Street
Brooklyn, NY 11222
(Visit their web site at www.grassrootsrenewal.com)

PRINTED IN THE UNITED STATES OF AMERICA

"Truly, truly, I say to you, when you were young, you girded yourself and walked where you would; but when you are old, you will stretch out your hands, and another will gird you and carry you where you do not wish to go." (This he said to show by what death he was to glorify God.) And after this he said to him, "Follow me."

JOHN 21:18-19

Contents

Preface *by Michael Dubruiel*   9

Introduction *by Father Glenn Sudano, C.F.R.*   11

PART ONE:
An Interview with Father Benedict Groeschel, C.F.R.,
by John Bishop

Introduction to Interview with Father Benedict   19
Franciscan Friars of the Renewal — C.F.R.   22
Crisis in the Church   25
Signs of Hope   28
Death and Purgatory   33
The Cross at Ground Zero — 9/11   38
Abortion   41
Where Is God When Bad Things Happen?   47
Atheism   53
Clergy and Sex   56
Father Benedict's Vocation   58
The Poor   65
Mother Teresa of Calcutta   69
John Paul the Great   75
Future Plans   78
Notes for Part One   81

PART TWO:
Reflections After the Accident,
by Father Benedict Groeschel, C.F.R.

Editor's Introduction to Father Benedict's Reflections 85
The Providence of God   87

There Are No Accidents   88

Wasted Pain   89

Gratitude   90

The Passion of Christ   91

Our Dependency on Christ   92

"I Am With You!"   93

God Still Wants You Here   94

Progress   95

Hope   96

Thanksgiving   97

Offering It Up!   99

"Thy Will Be Done"   100

Dealing With Setbacks   101

Keeping Faith   102

Time to Reflect   103

Hospitals and Faith   104

Reason to Be Happy   105

Instruments of God   106

Live by Love   108

Penance   109

Good Friday in a Hospital   110

Christ Is Risen!   111

Ask, "What Am I to Do?"   113

What God Permits   114

The Mystery of the Cross   115

Visiting the Sick   116

Death Is Never Far Away   117

Call of Divine Mercy   118

**How You Can Help the Franciscan
Friars of the Renewal**   119

Acknowledgments   123

Preface

On January 11, 2004, a car in Orlando, Florida, struck Father Benedict Groeschel and nearly took his life. I heard about the accident on the morning of January 12 when I arrived for work. News about Father's condition was slow in coming that morning, and like countless others that day who were shocked by the news, I did what I knew Father Benedict would want me to do — I prayed.

Later that same morning, as I was opening my mail, I found among the parcels I had received a large envelope from overseas. It contained a letter that began with the words "Father Benedict Groeschel, C.F.R., suggested that you might be interested in publishing this."

The "this" in question was a lengthy interview — book length — which the author John Bishop had conducted with Father Benedict. Reading it, I was reminded of the greatness of this humble friar and the difference that he and his religious community, the Franciscan Friars of the Renewal, have made in the Catholic Church in the United States and throughout the world.

As I read through the interview, I was struck with the irony of receiving it on the very day that Father had suddenly been silenced. I was also struck by how John Bishop had asked all the right questions. He covered every conceivable question that a Catholic living in the United States in the twenty-first century would like answered.

I have known Father Benedict for over twenty years — first as a Capuchin friar, and then as a co-founder of the Franciscan Friars of the Renewal. I have benefited from his wisdom while making individual retreats with him as well as participating in group retreats he has led. I have been blessed to work with him on two previous books that Our Sunday Visitor has published: *The Cross at Ground Zero*, which was a response to the attacks of 9/11; and *From Scandal to Hope*, a response to the current crisis in the Church. I have seen Father in action, and what he is able to accomplish on an average day is nothing short of miraculous. Even now, while recuperating from his injuries, he continues to reach out through the Friars' website with daily meditations drawn from his recovery in the hospital — meditations which are now in the book you hold in your hands.

Part One of this book contains the interview that I first read on the morning following Father Benedict's accident. Part Two consists of Father Benedict's reflections on his accident and recovery, and how this trying ordeal has validated all that he has preached to others throughout his years of ministry.

There is one part of the interview where John Bishop quizzes Father about how he came to start all the charitable enterprises he has taken up during his life. Father Benedict repeats his answer a number of times — "No plans, be led." Whatever God wants, Father Benedict will be led in that direction. Hopefully, you and I can learn that lesson too. As Father has said since the accident, "There are no accidents." May this great man's faith help you and me to trust in God ever more, no matter what may happen!

MICHAEL DUBRUIEL
Acquisitions Editor
Our Sunday Visitor
Divine Mercy Sunday
April 18, 2004

Introduction

Tragedy rarely creeps into our lives. Rather, it crashes through the roof suddenly and lands right in our lap. I will never forget the night when it suddenly descended and shattered the lively conversation and lighthearted laughter at a dinner table three months ago.

On January 11, 2004, Father Benedict flew to Florida after completing a preaching engagement in California. He arrived at the Orlando International Airport with his traveling companions, David Burns and Father John Lynch. They left the airport terminal and travelled the short distance to the car rental site to pick up a rental car. Father Benedict knew his two weary companions hadn't eaten dinner, and looking at the long line of customers before them, he decided to slip away and get something for them to eat.

The details of what happened next are not clear, but many can tell you that accidents at airports are not uncommon. Between the fast traffic and poor lighting, many pedestrians have been injured or killed around airports. This night it was Father Benedict's turn to discover how quickly a tragedy like this can happen.

While crossing a street, Father was struck by a vehicle on his right side. The impact shattered his right arm and broke his leg in two places. He also received a head injury that initially appeared much worse than it actually was. Both divine mercy and providence deigned that the accident occur only minutes away from the Orlando Regional Medical Center, which has a first-rate trauma unit.

The night of the accident, I was in California with the friars from St. Felix Friary. We were there to conduct a youth retreat at a friar's home parish. When I received the call from Father Conrad in New York, we were relaxing, laughing, and sitting around the table enjoying a home-cooked meal. The terrible news came as a bolt out of the blue. The solemn tone of Father Conrad's voice underscored the fact that Father Benedict's injuries were serious — very serious. After hanging up the phone, I told everyone at the table the terrible news. Within seconds, our forks were flat on the table and our Rosaries in hand. This was the beginning of a long and fear-filled night, lying awake most of the time with a cordless phone in my hand. Morning finally came, and I was off to the airport with bloodshot eyes and a heavy, heavy heart.

On the plane, my mind kept creeping down a dark road. I couldn't help imagining the worst. I thought that God was certainly giving us some time to prepare ourselves for the worst. I kept thinking, "I'm not strong enough to accept the cross. The community isn't ready." Yet, within me was also a subtle voice that called me to continue to pray. I remember saying to myself, "Is it a sin to hope? Isn't hope something the Lord calls us to?" Yes, although my feelings went one way, my will went the other. I felt like going downhill, down that dark road, but I chose to climb the steep hill of hope. In fact, if a book could be written about the entire affair — the accident, the recovery, the healing — I would call it *A Drama of Hope*.

In the days and weeks that followed, there were periods filled with both dark clouds, which would roll in quickly, and short sudden bursts of sunlight. Because of Father's age and previous medical conditions, especially his bad heart, everything was "touch and go."

I continually asked the nurses, "How is he doing?"

They would look back with concerned eyes and pursed lips and say, "He's a very sick man, Father."

I couldn't easily control my imagination. One hour I would "see" the friars around his graveside, and the next hour we would be marching with him to the altar for a Mass of Thanksgiving. I was full of fear and full of hope. I learned the two can walk hand-in-hand, just as long as hope leads the other feelings along.

As the first days of recovery crept along, a story of faith, hope, and love began to emerge. Not a day went by without some sign, some message, or some indication that God was near. Because Father was highly sedated, he could not utter a single word, yet those of us who daily surrounded his bed spoke to him, encouraged him, and of course prayed with him.

In time, the doctors permitted the friars to celebrate Mass in the room. Although these Masses were brief and completely unadorned, they were powerful and full of meaning. One friar told me, "Father's like the host on the paten being offered up." Although he was not able to utter the words "This is My Body, this is My Blood," he was indeed celebrating the Mass perhaps more than he ever had in the past or ever will in the future.

As the weeks progressed, Father Benedict slowly — very slowly — came out of the medicated "fog" he had been wandering in since the night of the accident. Although the drugs kept his body still and far from pain, they would induce frightful dreams which he later related to us. When he was finally able to speak, he told me about a "nightmare" he'd had. I thought he was going to talk about monsters or demons. But instead he said, "I had a terrible, terrible dream. I was in a place with many poor people who needed my help, and I was unable to do a thing!"

After he told me about this "nightmare," I thought to myself, "My God, he's even concerned about the poor in his dreams!" Although I kept silent, I was deeply concerned about the import of his frightful dreams.

As the weeks wore on, each day brought certain signs of hope. Although Father could not speak due to a tracheotomy, he was able to communicate. At first, it took some time to understand what he was saying, yet every attempt to "speak" revealed that despite his head injury, his mind was still sharp. Every nurse or attendant who walked into his room received his attention. He would feebly raise his broken and bandaged arm to get their attention. Then he would mouth the words "What is your name?" or "Where are you from?" We were amazed that he remembered everything. Since many of the hospital help were from faraway places, like the Philippines or India, he would smile and mouth the words "I've been there." His well-known and wonderful ability to connect and be concerned for others, especially the common person, was not affected by his evident pain.

If there is anything to be said about Father Benedict and this terrible chapter in his life, it is this — he practices what he preaches. In a time when there has been so much distrust and disappointment in religion, Father Benedict has displayed an authenticity and fidelity that many people thought had died and disappeared. The powerful sermons he has preached with his lips are now lived out in his life. It simply takes skill in oratory to preach effectively to people, but it takes real faith to live the message. He has preached to millions about perseverance in suffering, hope during desperate situations, and trust during deepest darkness. Now every word has been painfully tried and proven true.

While there is much of the story still to be told, I am thankful that, at the time of this writing, Father Benedict is well on the road to the healing of his many wounds. Each day, he is literally taking steps on the road to full recovery. Perhaps he will be seen less at airports, but he certainly will be seen by many more on television. Michael Dubruiel, the acquisitions editor at Our Sunday Visitor who brought this book about — as well as a friend of Father Benedict's — will be happy to hear that Father plans to be "running less and writing more."

It is of interest to note that on the day of the accident, Michael received the manuscript of the interview that Father had done with John Bishop which is included in this book. The interview, contained in Part One of this book, covers a wide range of topics, but written between the lines is the message that everything Father Benedict speaks of he also deeply believes — and lives. Thanks be to God, you can also read in Part Two of this book Father's own thoughts about suffering and the accident that nearly took him from us. It is easy to talk *about* the holy Gospel, it is another thing to *live* it.

Father Benedict has been severely tried and tested in his many months of recovery, like gold "tested by fire" (1 Peter 1:7) or silver "purified seven times" (Psalm 12:6), as the Scriptures would put it. How wonderful it is to know that God in His mercy has allowed him to remain with us. Like the Holy Father, he is preaching more by example than with words — showing us that God is faithful and loving even in darkness, pain, illness, and injury. Most assuredly, we can imagine that God's mercy is being made manifest, permitting these two great lights to shine ever more brightly in a dark, dark world.

Finally, I want to thank the Mother of God, who since that first and frightful night has never left my side or the broken side of Father Benedict. How grateful I am, together with all the friars, for the millions of prayers offered by so many for Father's welfare. So here we see, right in our midst, how much she deserves the title "Mother of Mercy." To her, and to you,

the reader who is proud to call Father Benedict "friend," I am
deeply, deeply grateful.

FR. GLENN SUDANO, C.F.R.
Community Servant (superior)
Franciscan Friars of the Renewal
Feast of St. Benedict Joseph Labré
April 16, 2004

PART ONE

An Interview with
Father Benedict Groeschel, C.F.R.,
by John Bishop

INTRODUCTION TO INTERVIEW
WITH FATHER BENEDICT

I had a very difficult time finding the right words to introduce this interview. Father Benedict is a man who wears many hats. He is a founder of an order of Franciscans under the authority of the Holy See, the director for the Office of Spiritual Development of the Archdiocese of New York, a professor of pastoral psychology at Saint Joseph's Seminary, and the founder of Trinity Retreat, a center for prayer and study for the clergy. More recently, Father Benedict has become a member of the governing board of Ave Maria University, a Catholic institution of higher education which is being established in Florida and which, I venture to predict, will have a major impact on the restoration of the Church within the United States and throughout the world. On top of all this, he is also an internationally known lecturer and retreat master, a prolific author, and a star of EWTN (Eternal Word Television Network), although he prefers to be called a "regular guest."

As you will see in the interview, he is very capable of expressing himself. In the tradition of St. Francis, however, he would not welcome a great trumpet blast of adulation from an interviewer he has just met — although he is worthy of much adulation. With this in mind, let me just list some of the achievements or, as Father prefers to call them, "works of love" which he and his friars, along with their friends and benefactors, have established in the Bronx and other poor parts of the metropolitan New York area. Since the community was started in April of 1987, they have set up the Padre Pio Shelter, the St. Crispin Food Pantry, the St. Francis Center, the St. Anthony Residence, the St. Francis House, Our Lady of Guadalupe Convent (where the Franciscan Sisters of the Renewal reside), and Casa Juan Diego, which is a religious and social centre for Hispanic immigrant workers — young, single Mexican-Americans, who have no other support in the area. The friars also support the Good Counsel Homes for homeless mothers and assist expectant mothers, homeless men, emotionally disturbed boys, and the families of those in prison.

As if they didn't have enough to do at home, the friars have also established ministries abroad. In the summer, they go to Bosnia to rebuild homes for the needy people of that war-torn territory. And just to keep busy, in April of 2000 the friars began a program and center for the poor in Canning Town, London, England. Post-Christian Britain will be a tough nut to crack, but I have no doubt as to their ultimate success. That same year, they also opened a mission for the poor in the poorest country in Latin America, Honduras.

Father Benedict's order performs all of these services without regard to race, creed, or color. They care for Christians, Jews, Muslims, Hindus, Buddhists, agnostics, and atheists, and they are entirely supported by charity.

All this work is carried out by a modest number of friars and sisters. But what recruits! Let me paint a word picture for you. On the front page of *Grayfriar News* (Issue 21, Winter 2000) is a black-and-white photograph. Two large muscular men, one sporting an impressive black beard and the other a small goatee, both in their late twenties or early thirties — the prime of life — are lounging on a sofa with their arms filled with children. Six youngsters are in the photograph. The caption reads: "On Sundays, student friars like Brother Joseph Mary Dean and Brother Anthony Marie Baetzold take a break from the books and enjoy visiting families.

This *Grayfriar* photo shows the friars kept quite busy thanks to the Rosado children who live near the friars in the Bronx." Get the picture?

Before turning to the interview, I'd better mention Father Bernard Murphy, Father Benedict's fellow almoner and companion in the great work. I don't want to incur Father Benedict's displeasure by leaving his friend out.

Now I can proceed with the interview. Father Benedict is warm. He is witty. He is wise. But he also has a certain steel in his eyes!

JOHN BISHOP

FRANCISCAN FRIARS
OF THE RENEWAL — C.F.R.

JOHN BISHOP: Father, first of all I want to know about the initials "C.F.R.," the designation of your order.

FATHER BENEDICT: Yes. Well, about fifteen years ago, eight of us who were Capuchins decided that, because of the way that things were going in religious life and in the Church, we would leave the Capuchins and start a new community to work exclusively with the poor — to live with the poor and to preach. The special emphases of our community are loyalty to the Holy Father, devotion to the presence of Christ in the Eucharist, devotion to the Blessed Mother and the saints, and particularly a loyalty to the Catholic interpretation of the Bible, the dogmas of the Church, and the traditions of the Church.

As you know, St. Francis made it a point that a part of his life would be an observance of the Gospel. So from the Missionaries of Charity, from Mother Teresa, we learned the daily Eucharistic Holy Hour. We celebrate the offices of the Church and our prayers. Our community is located in the slums. Our first house is in the South Bronx; we have a place in Harlem; we are in a poor section of Yonkers; we are in the East End of London; and there is a very poor little place — it is in a small city — in Honduras.

We are hoping, in the relatively near future perhaps, to open in France, where we will work with the homeless, especially with the Muslims. We are hoping to get something going there.

JOHN BISHOP: Ah, yes, there is a very long tradition of Franciscans trying to approach Muslims.

FATHER BENEDICT: There is indeed.

JOHN BISHOP: St. Francis of Assisi himself went to the Holy Land.

FATHER BENEDICT: Yes. He went to the Holy Land himself. And he is said to have spoken to the sultan.

JOHN BISHOP: Father, are you still Franciscans?

FATHER BENEDICT: Oh, yes. We left to set up our new community, and our sponsor was Cardinal O'Connor. Initially we had hoped to be a jurisdiction under the Capuchin General, and the General went along with that at the request of the Holy See. The Holy See backed us one hundred percent, but the Capuchin provincials in the United States voted not to allow us to stay.

JOHN BISHOP: Why?

FATHER BENEDICT: Well, I could understand that. We were obviously being critical of the status quo. Some of the provincials were friends of mine and they told me we would do better if we were out. So we have grown very exponentially, really. We now have eighty friars and eleven sisters. We have a separate community of sisters. We work very much like the Missionaries of Charity. The proper name is the "Community of the Franciscans of the Renewal". We are expecting fifteen more postulants in the fall of 2002.

JOHN BISHOP: Right. But is there not something more to that? What was the problem that caused you to move out?

FATHER BENEDICT: Well, it was the general scene in religious life in the United States, and I described much of this in a book entitled *The Reform of the Renewal* (Ignatius Press, 1990), which I wrote shortly after we left. I think it could be summarized by saying that there was a decline in Catholic education, a catastrophic decline, particularly in seminary education and in higher education. There was loss of a loyalty to the dogmatic teaching of the church, a great deal of confusion in moral theology, and a great deal of skepticism about Scripture. And together with this, many religious orders seemed to have lost their way. There was a catastrophic decline in vocations, and you can see we have not had that decline. We have grown very quickly. I am the only "old" man in the whole community. The average age is about thirty-one. So if I drop dead it will go down to twenty nine! [*Chuckles from both.*]

CRISIS IN THE CHURCH

JOHN BISHOP: Father, how free are you — let me put it that way — to talk about what is called the "crisis in the Catholic Church" at this time in our history?

FATHER BENEDICT: Oh, I am free in the sense that nobody is going to contradict me if I tell the truth. I don't want to paint the picture too black, because there are endless numbers of clergy and laity and members of the hierarchy who are very devout and good Christians, who I think are working to get us out of the mess. I think the biggest problem is to convince them that they are ill. This is so often the most difficult.

JOHN BISHOP: So for someone like me, Father, sometimes troubled because I span the old Church and the so-called new Church, and I watch bishops not doing their duty in various parts of the world, and I watch laity becoming more and more upset because it seems that the divinity of Christ is being played down if it is even mentioned at all; the Holy Mass is being turned into a memorial meal, and there is evidence of this. So what do we do? Do we have to end up staying at home on Sundays reading the Gospel for the day?

FATHER BENEDICT: Well, let's take it a piece at a time. A great deal of this, the decline in the belief in the divinity of Christ, comes from the abuse of the historical-critical method Scripture scholarship. The method itself may not be defective. I suspect that it is. It is not particularly scientific. It is supposed to be scientific, but that claim is made by people who have never studied science. It does not follow the scientific method at all. It is constantly talking about what didn't happen. In science you never attempt to prove something did not happen. That is a negative hypothesis. So it is very deficient as regards the science. Also, anybody who knows the scientific method knows that it is theoretical. You may have an answer today that you reject tomorrow. There are other defects too, like the absence of probability.

JOHN BISHOP: Yes, yes.

FATHER BENEDICT: All you have to have for a theory is that it covers all the cases in the universe that you are talking about and that it be self-consistent. So I blame many of the problems of this method on Rudolf Bultmann, a German Scripture scholar, a Lutheran, and one who has been rapped in a recent statement of the Pontifical Biblical Commission of the Church. And he deserves it. His influence was particularly strong in Germany, since he was a Lutheran pastor.

JOHN BISHOP: When you say, "rapped," you mean he was rapped over the knuckles?

FATHER BENEDICT: Yes. He was very severely called into question. But a great many people followed Bultmann for a long, long time. And I think foolishly. I won't go extensively into Bultmann, but let me give you an example. Cardinal Schonborn, Cardinal/Archbishop of Vienna, invited me to give a retreat to the priests of the Archdiocese of Vienna. He asked me what I was going to give the retreat on, and I answered, "Devotion to Jesus Christ."

He said, "You could not have chosen a better topic because Christ has all but disappeared in Western Europe."

JOHN BISHOP: That is quite right.

FATHER BENEDICT: But it is not the case in the United States. Devotion is growing. On the part of young people in the U.S.A., there is an incredible restoration of devotion to Christ, faith in the Gospels, faith in the Christian life and tradition.

JOHN BISHOP: But how has that come about? Because in Europe we would like to have the recipe!

FATHER BENEDICT: Purely by the gifts of the Holy Spirit. I don't think there is any human means that could possibly explain it.

JOHN BISHOP: What about activities such as yours? Shrug aside modesty, Father.

FATHER BENEDICT: No, no. We responded to it. We didn't cause it.

SIGNS OF HOPE

JOHN BISHOP: EWTN (Eternal Word Television Network). How instrumental has that been?

FATHER BENEDICT: Well, EWTN preserves the Catholic tradition very strongly, and I have been a part of EWTN, and honored to be so, for eighteen years. But I have been teaching in the seminary since 1965, which was before the Council, so I have gone through the whole earthquake, and I have been thrown out of four seminaries, two of which no longer exist.[1]

JOHN BISHOP: Badges of honor?

FATHER BENEDICT: Well, I have been thrown out of better places! The fact is that for years I was trying to convince seminarians of the truth of the Faith, and now I don't have to do that at all. They convince me before I open my mouth. They don't know the truth of the Faith but they are waiting there with bated breath for me to give it to them.

JOHN BISHOP: Well, it is miraculous, then.

FATHER BENEDICT: It is. It is absolutely a gift of the Holy Spirit.

JOHN BISHOP: Yes, bearing in mind the school system and the whole works.

FATHER BENEDICT: And what is emerging, as I have mentioned in the book *The New Faithful*, by Colleen Carroll, from Loyola University Press in Chicago ...

JOHN BISHOP: A book about [*reading out loud*] "why young adults are embracing Christian orthodoxy."

FATHER BENEDICT: Yes.

JOHN BISHOP: Loyola Press?

FATHER BENEDICT: Loyola Press, of all people. The very press that published a book ten years ago by a priest who resigned from the priesthood during a homosexual meeting, and who spent five pages denouncing me in his book.

JOHN BISHOP: I have hunted down another great priest for a book that I am working on, a Jesuit who — and I say this, not he — has been disgracefully treated by some of his confreres because of his unswerving faith and loyalty to the teaching of the Church. I am sure he bears the slights as badges of honor as well.

FATHER BENEDICT: Two years ago, I wrote a letter to the Father General of the Jesuits, because my father and all my uncles on both sides are Jesuit graduates — my mother's brothers, my father's brothers. One of my great uncles worked all of his life as an employee of the Society of Jesus. So I have some Jesuit credentials. My relatives expected me to be a Jesuit, but I wanted to work for the poor and I love St. Francis.

I wrote to the Father General and told him everyplace I go I run into young Jesuits despondent and heartbroken — seminarians and young priests — because of lack of loyalty to the Catholic tradition and lack of loyalty to the Holy Father. He wrote me back and said he knew there was a problem, but he thought I might have been overstating it. I was thinking of sending him a postcard back saying, "How do you know?" But it isn't just the Jesuits. It is all over the place.

However, the new orders are very different — the Community of St. John in France, the Fraternity of St. Peter, the Legionaries of Christ, and the Franciscans of the Immaculate. Then there are the Sisters of Life, founded by Cardinal O'Connor. And we are growing together here in New York. When he was dying, Cardinal O'Connor asked me to be responsible for their financial well-being. Then there are the Sisters of Mary Mother of the Church, founded by Mother Assumpta out in Michigan, who are doing very well.

So there are new orders everywhere. They are all the same. They all wear the habit. They are intensely loyal to the Catholic faith, to the Holy Father. They all love Christ in the Blessed Sacrament. They might be quite different in other ways, but in essentials they are the same.

JOHN BISHOP: Father, before we move on — I know you are a psychologist by training — let me ask you this question: Why, in the Church, did the "left" persist in being "left" long after those so-called "Christian Marxist/Leninist" theories had been discredited in practice? Why, in our Church, have some persisted in this failed policy?

FATHER BENEDICT: Well, at least in the United States, not too many were politically left. They may have been more liberal, but they certainly weren't Marxist. You might still see some in Latin America. Probably the only authentic Marxists left in the world are a few priests and nuns in Latin America. There certainly aren't any in China! If Marx came back from the dead, he would haunt them all! I have never seen so much state capitalism in my life as in China.

But, you see, Catholics are the last to get off the deck of a burning ship. It is an occupational hazard. The actual fact is that what has come to judgment in the crisis in the Church right now was not so much a sociological or political liberalism as a theological liberalism.

This liberalism can be defined, following Cardinal Newman, as "belief without content." When Cardinal Newman was given the letter, the *biletto*, announcing that he had been made a Cardinal by Pope Leo, the oratorians were gathered there at the Birmingham Oratory and they waited for him to say something. He said, "All of my life I have opposed liberalism." That was his statement. He was speaking about theological liberalism, not sociological liberalism. In fact he was a friend of the liberal Prime Minister Gladstone. But in theology, liberalism has come to mean belief without content. So someone will say, "I believe in Jesus. But I don't know what I believe."

JOHN BISHOP: That is an extraordinary state of mind, isn't it? I would have thought that intelligent people holding that view would just have to leave the Church. I mean, if I lost my faith I would have to leave the Church. I couldn't practice anymore.

FATHER BENEDICT: Well, they haven't lost it, but they don't know what it means. Or they have rejected what it means. You know, to be very stupid you have to be very intelligent. Normal stupidity only requires normal intelligence. But great stupidity requires a good deal of mental equipment and perspicacity and even dedication to a cause. So, to be very stupid you have to be very, very smart. And most of the very stupid things that have ever been done in human history have been done by very smart people: Caesar, Napoleon ... Perhaps one of the stupid people who really did something awful was Hitler. He was just generally stupid, giftedly stupid. But the rest of them were moderately intelligent and stupid. That is what is going on right now.

People are unduly disturbed because they don't know enough Church history. We have gone through this before. In the Renaissance, the Capuchins, to which we belonged, were founded in 1535, ten years before the Council of Trent. Then, there were the Jesuits and the Carmelite reform. There were all kinds of ills and abuses and then reforms. But the fact is that we will go through trials and the gates of hell cannot prevail against the Church. I am rather happy to be getting ready to get out of here.

DEATH AND PURGATORY

JOHN BISHOP: How do you mean, Father?

FATHER BENEDICT: Well, I am seventy!

JOHN BISHOP: Oh, I see [*chuckling*]. Oh, I don't think He is going to let you go just yet.

FATHER BENEDICT: Well it says in the Scriptures the length of our lives is seventy years, or eighty if we are strong, and I have never been strong. I had polio when I was a kid. But I said to the brothers on my fiftieth anniversary that I am looking forward enthusiastically to purgatory and would happily go now.

JOHN BISHOP: Oh, yes, Father. Purgatory. You mentioned in one of your books that if we get there we might be able to ask questions.

FATHER BENEDICT: Oh, yes, I am planning on that.

JOHN BISHOP: Well, that's great. Because I thought it was only if we made it to heaven we might be able to ask Him all sorts of things. You know, "How did You create the heavens and the earth?" That sort of thing.

FATHER BENEDICT: You wouldn't give a hoot! We go to heaven with the Holy Spirit, who searches the things of God. We wouldn't need to ask Him any questions.

JOHN BISHOP: So there, in heaven, we will be free of that kind of burden, of needing to know?

FATHER BENEDICT: But in purgatory there are several things. Why are there volcanoes? Why are there earthquakes? Why are there brussels sprouts! [*Laughter*]

St. Catherine of Genoa says that the joy of the souls in purgatory is exceeded only by the joy of the saints in heaven. Purgatory has been given a bad name. St. Catherine of Genoa is the great mystic of purgatory and one of the guiding lights of my life. She was the Mother Teresa of her time, but St. Catherine was a lay woman. She had the answer. She was running the largest hospital in the world for poor people during the pontificate of Alexander VI, who probably did not make it to purgatory.[2] If he did, he will probably be there long after the apocalypse as part of the clean-up crew! But I have some things to say about what I think Catherine did. Catherine started the Catholic Reformation almost thirty years before the Protestant Reformation.

American Protestants of the "Holiness Movement," a spiritual revival in the nineteenth century, read the works of Catherine of Genoa and published her. They called her, "Madame Adorno." She wrote, "And God stands at the open gates of heaven summoning the souls with looks of great love. But they will not come in unless they are completely purified."

As my friend Frank Sheed said about purgatory, "The very thought of appearing before the Divine Majesty in my present unseemly state fills me with horror." Now what we have to do, and this is my point, is that we have to work as they did then for the reform of the Church. There is much vitality in the Church coming from the Holy Spirit.

It is a delight to me to teach young people today because they believe before they hear. They want me to tell them what the Faith is, rather than what I went through for twenty-five years, of trying to convince them as to what the Faith is. Remember, I did not teach theology directly. But I taught pastoral counseling and spirituality. I got fired from various places because I would insist on putting in Catholic theology as a background to counseling and psychology. Had I been a theologian, I probably wouldn't have been hired at all. Now I see the great change coming in this country and beginning in England.

JOHN BISHOP: Really? [*Astounded*] In England?

FATHER BENEDICT: We have eight English brothers. We participate in "Youth 2000," going on all over the place, and we have lots of support from the clergy because it works. Modern people like things that work.

JOHN BISHOP: What you are doing, say I wickedly, is you're doing the work that the bishops in the United Kingdom should have set up years ago.

FATHER BENEDICT: It wasn't clear then that you could get this response from youth. I have worked with priests and bishops for thirty years full-time, John, and I am by no means as critical of bishops as other people are. I know that they were cast into a role for which they were totally unprepared, because the role of bishops changed dramatically at the Vatican Council. Whereas, before, bishops could be rather direct — and, if you will, autocratic, or at least hierarchically pastoral — they were suddenly expected to consult with everybody and to try to keep everybody happy. They came home from the Council not trained to do that: to try to be benevolent and kind and understanding. And what happened, unfortunately, was that the sense of sin went out the window.

Then we had the culture of dissent — which, as George Weigel points out so well, came from the rejection of the papal teaching in *Humanae Vitae* on contraception.[3] Once dissent can come in on one important teaching, it can come in on everything else.

But I know the bishops here. At one point five years ago, I had given retreats to one fifth of all the bishops in the United States. People would say to me, "Oh, you have to tell the bishops off. You have got to yell at the bishops. Bawl 'em out." The poor men would get out of the bus or the van and no one, with normal wit or talent, would have shouted at these people because they needed first aid.

My Irish great-grandmother, Susie Murphy, used to make a very sage remark: "The people get the clergy they deserve." You see, the people get the clergy they deserve, the people get the clergy they produce, and they got the bishops they wanted. And the bishops worried that they had to be what many people wanted.

JOHN BISHOP: Oh, yes, that's right.

FATHER BENEDICT: Don't just blame the bishops. If you had a tough bishop who called people to order, he would have had a revolution on his hands. It happened at various places. So I don't think people should single out the bishops. They have a great responsibility. And I don't think people should single out the clergy, either. I think we all bear a responsibility. And I don't think the lay people should be singled out. We are all in this together. Many times the people got what they wanted from a priest.

In the scandal over here,[4] the occasion of removing a number of priests from office set off gigantic protests among the laity, who didn't want them removed, because the priests had repented years and years ago and they were popular priests. Catholic priests in the United States have been very popular, and that popularity is surviving the media blitz against the Church. I am hoping that what will happen is that we will realize that we need a reform.

THE CROSS AT GROUND ZERO — 9/11

JOHN BISHOP: We look forward to that, Father. Now, let's dip into your book entitled *The Cross at Ground Zero* (Our Sunday Visitor, 2001). In it, you write, "Religion should be prepared to be unpopular." You say that.

FATHER BENEDICT: Yes, I certainly believe that.

JOHN BISHOP: So what price your "popular" priests?

FATHER BENEDICT: Well, you see, they weren't told that. That's my statement. You see, if a priest came down a bit too hard, the complaint went to the chancery, and most of the time the chancery would call the priest in and . . .

JOHN BISHOP: Yes, that has been a sickening feature. Imagine Catholic people doing what Shakespeare described as the "telling of the King" in *Richard the Third*. Running behind the back of someone and "tittle-tattling" to authority — telling on their priest for doing his job properly.

FATHER BENEDICT: But you see, that was the understanding of the democratizing Church. I think the Church lost the sense of the pastoral office. It lost it in the seminary. Nobody sat in a dark room and planned this out. It not only happened in the Catholic Church; it happened in the other major denominations. I understand it happened in the Scottish Kirk, and if it could happen there it could happen anywhere.

JOHN BISHOP: Well, that's right. Now a brief, crude critique of your book *The Cross at Ground Zero*.

FATHER BENEDICT: I'll probably agree with you.

JOHN BISHOP: Now you don't say that the disaster of September 11, 2001, happened because the United States is a cesspit, but you do say that Americans should consider their position, having been confronted with this enormous tragedy. You do say things like, "the public media is a septic tank."

FATHER BENEDICT: I was being quite charitable, actually!

JOHN BISHOP: Is it that bad? Because, as you know, we are visiting the U.S.A., and much of what we have seen on the TV screens here is pure as the driven snow compared with what is transmitted in Britain nightly.

FATHER BENEDICT: Well, I guess what you would say is it is a decline in society in the western world. Because, after all, sexual morality, among its many purposes, is the protection of family life. That is a very high, primary responsibility. Family life is decaying everywhere. The cause is the naïveté of the pro-abortion group, and particularly Planned Parenthood. They not only have done everything possible to undermine the sacredness of life, but have done everything to undermine sexual morality.

Then there are the media. Someone did a study in California about five years ago among 200,000 media people. I don't remember whom that included. I suppose they ranged from the owners of the companies down to the "best boy" on the set. About ninety-two percent of them were in favor of abortion on demand; about ninety-four percent of them favored the public acceptance of homosexual relationships. So they are not particularly favorable to us.

Now on the other hand, statistics show that in the United States ninety-four percent believe in a personal God, ninety-two percent believe that you are going to meet Him when you get out of this place and render an account, and eighty-six percent of the American people believe that Jesus Christ is the Son of God. Now they might not have the slightest idea of what that means. It is faith without content.

ABORTION

JOHN BISHOP: Now, Father, I was appalled to read that you were actually imprisoned, together with an eighty-three-year-old bishop, for a peaceful act of protest.

FATHER BENEDICT: We were saying the Rosary.

JOHN BISHOP: Right. It was outside an abortion clinic. Now let me act the role of, let us say, a county court judge. He arraigns you before the court and he says something like this: "Listen, you people. We have had a murder in this country some time back. Okay, you Catholics didn't kill that abortionist doctor. It was somebody else; a Protestant nut. But we have to be very careful. You Catholic priests come along — you are kind of terrorists-in-waiting. We have to act tough. Otherwise, we are going to have someone else who comes along and shoots another abortionist." Comments?

FATHER BENEDICT: That was not what happened. The judge who sent us to prison was a convert to the Catholic Church, a nice old lady. I had known her for years. She was under the instruction of the deputy of the local federal attorney. We purposely disobeyed the police instruction. You can say the Rosary outside an abortion clinic, but you can't stand still when you say it.

JOHN BISHOP: And you can't kneel down.

FATHER BENEDICT: No. So we knelt down in the driveway, and the police officers read the riot act to us, and we remained in an act of disobedience. I was familiar with civil disobedience, being a veteran of the civil rights movement for many years. Civil disobedience is not a thing you should do easily, but it can be an effective tool. The Holy Father called for it in his encyclical *Evangelium Vitae*.

So I got five days; Brother Fidelis, now in Canning Town, London, England, got ten, and the late Bishop George Lynch got fifteen days because he had been arrested so many times. Now I didn't mind being arrested. We had signed up. But it was how we were treated in prison. This is a largely Catholic area. Most of the prison guards and officials are Catholic.

JOHN BISHOP: So this happened in the New York area?

FATHER BENEDICT: It happened here in Westchester County, which is an affluent area in New York State, probably forty or fifty percent Catholic. We were strip-searched three times in twenty-four hours, and there were various other indignities. The prisoners were extremely kind. They didn't know we were priests, but they knew we were old. So we were called "Pop". "Get your sandwiches over there, Pop", they would say. They were very nice. The prison doctor was a gentleman. The guards were disgraceful; I complained.

JOHN BISHOP: Catholic guards?

FATHER BENEDICT: One of them volunteered the information that he had graduated from Cardinal Hayes High School. I said to him, "You did this to a bishop of the Catholic Church. You better watch out."

He said, "Well, it's the rule."

And I said, "Yeah, and it's the rule in this prison that there is no marijuana too!"

Now I don't blame the guards. They were doing what they were told, but the whole system rots as far as I am concerned.

JOHN BISHOP: Now one of the priests had some vestments . . .

FATHER BENEDICT: That was Father Conrad. He was in jail for a year.

JOHN BISHOP: Same incident?

FATHER BENEDICT: No, no; he and others went into a clinic and broke up some equipment in Pennsylvania. And they didn't sign a document that they wouldn't do it again. It is a mistake in one sense, but you know on the other hand abortionists are killing people. If you were walking past a house and a woman came to window and shouted, "I'm being murdered," you would break in and try to save her. But of course the abortionists are simply murdering babies. You see, the voice of religion in this country, of all religious denominations in this country, has been pathetic. The voice of the Catholic hierarchy has been the loudest.

JOHN BISHOP: But has it? I have a dream, like Martin Luther King, that not only the American hierarchy, but the English one as well, would get up as a body and say, "Every Sunday we are going to march through the streets in an old-fashioned Blessed Sacrament-style procession. It is going to be against the killing of babies by abortionists." This, coupled with the bishops speaking out at every opportunity and using every means of communication they could buy or muster. Why are they hiding away? They are letting priests like you go to prison. Why aren't they going to prison? At least one or two of them should go.

FATHER BENEDICT: Well, I was with a bishop.

JOHN BISHOP: Yes, of course, you were, but what about a hierarchical bishop, someone in charge of something.

FATHER BENEDICT: Well, there are diocesan bishops who have gone to prison.

JOHN BISHOP: What about the chairman of the U.S. or U.K. Conference of Bishops? What about a cardinal?

FATHER BENEDICT: Well, Cardinal Cooke was chairman of the Bishops' Committee on Pro-Life. He was very outspoken. So was Cardinal O'Connor.

JOHN BISHOP: Am I being unfair?

FATHER BENEDICT: I would think so. You are not a bishop. You know, things look different when you are there. You tend to get along with public officials. That is a tradition of the Church when it is accepted. Perhaps the best thing that could happen to the Church in the United States and in England is that it be persecuted.

JOHN BISHOP: Well, that's right.

FATHER BENEDICT: Then the bishops wouldn't have to get along with public officials.

JOHN BISHOP: You know, Father, some of the laity believe that they are being persecuted by their bishops — denied the full truth of the Faith.

FATHER BENEDICT: On the other hand, if the bishops did what you wanted, some of the laity would feel that they were being betrayed by the bishops too.

JOHN BISHOP: You mean the pro-abortion group within the Church?

FATHER BENEDICT: I wouldn't say the pro-abortion group, but the more liberal group of people. A bishop is in a tough spot. He has to be the "mostest of the mostest." I will tell you the people I am most critical of. Not the parish priest; parish priests have the obligation to "not break a bruised reed or quench a smoldering wick" (Matthew 12:20). They have that obligation. You can't get up in a parish and preach a stirring sermon against abortion and really bring out its horrors when you have four people sitting there in front of you who have had abortions and who feel horribly guilty about it and it haunts them every day.

JOHN BISHOP: It is difficult. I understand that.

FATHER BENEDICT: You know you have people practicing contraception; you have people doing all kinds of things

JOHN BISHOP: But there are more ways to skin a cat.

FATHER BENEDICT: Yes. In that case, I think parish priests have to use a spoonful of sugar. But who doesn't have to? Well, those who are not parish priests, the religious-order priests. That is why I think the most serious responsibility here is on religious order priests and teachers.

JOHN BISHOP: Well thank God for those like you, Father. Has your order had a cantilever effect on other orders?

FATHER BENEDICT: We get tons of mail.

JOHN BISHOP: Are other orders doing it too? What about the Jesuits?

FATHER BENEDICT: Not yet, because they are all over the place theologically. But in every province I ever visit, there are men who come out and give us their support. The Jesuits in general are mixed up, but some of the finest priests in the United States, and the most loyal to the pope, are Jesuits.

WHERE IS GOD WHEN BAD THINGS HAPPEN?

JOHN BISHOP: Father, let's stay with your book *The Cross and Ground Zero*, and ask the question so many were asking when the suicide planes struck on September 11, 2001: "Where was God when the towers crashed?"

FATHER BENEDICT: God was busy and right there, of course. Human beings have free will. They can do bad things. Probably, unless there were some small children in the towers, every one of them had done some bad things in their lives and were permitted to do it.

What we have is a madness, a fanaticism, a "jihad," the belief that you can bring, on earth, heavenly paradise. There have been other people in the twentieth century who thought they could do that — Hitler, Stalin, Mao Tse-tung, Idi Amin. But God was there. St. Augustine says that "God does not cause evil; He causes that evil does not become the worst." That is in his *Soliloquies*.

My father was a civil engineer. He almost built the World Trade Center. He built Madison Square Garden, the Lincoln Center, the United Nations Building — many buildings. He was very disappointed that his company did not get that contract. He would tell you that the World Trade Center was not a building, it was a tent; a glass and metal tent. Modern buildings are like that. They are not built of lasting material like stone. If you have ever seen photographs of the aftermath of an earthquake such as at Anchorage, Alaska, there are several buildings that remained together but were toppled sideways. They were leaning against one another looking like model buildings on a toy-train set. So those Twin Towers could have come over — fallen over on their sides — and killed 30,000.

John Bishop: Is that how many were in there at the time?

Father Benedict: There were more people in there, and if the sides had just fallen over they would have killed many people on the ground.

There were many people who did not arrive that day. A friend of mine was on the subway. She was a little bit late. They got to Fourteenth Street. She was on her way to the World Trade Center. The police stopped all the trains and had reversed all the escalators. She wasn't meant to be there.

John Bishop: So you are saying it was the restraining hand of God in operation?

Father Benedict: Oh, I don't think there was any doubt that it was. Look, you are talking to me and you are British. When you were a little boy, did you live through the Blitz?

John Bishop: Oh, yes.

Father Benedict: Well, I have a friend who was in London in 1942, Christmas Day, when Hitler dropped 15,000 incendiary bombs. Life goes on. Now I suppose it is difficult if you belong to some religion other than Christianity. Except Judaism; Judaism says, "Don't ask. God loves me."

John Bishop: Well . . . after the war a lot of people left the Jewish faith, saying He had deserted them in the camps.

FATHER BENEDICT: But those who did not leave said, "Don't ask."

JOHN BISHOP: That is even stricter than Catholicism.

FATHER BENEDICT: Well, that is from Job: "Who am I that I should ask?" In Christianity, you have the suffering God, the dying God. You know, some of our brothers were among the first down there at the Twin Towers. They went there on the fire engines.

JOHN BISHOP: You were working in the morgue as well, weren't you?

FATHER BENEDICT: The archdiocese kept two priests there for weeks. I was there voluntarily. The night I was there, eight remains were brought in. Only one was a body. The rest were in bags; decaying tissue. But it was 3,000 people. There were nights in London when more than 3,000 people died. In Dresden, in that war (World War II), 130,000 died in one night.

JOHN BISHOP: So we mustn't be blasé about it, but I might add, thousands of people die in Africa every month from state-induced terror, AIDS, crime, hunger, and gang warfare. We who have lived in Africa have lived with terror for many years.

FATHER BENEDICT: Yes, and remember 3,000 children a day die in the United States.

JOHN BISHOP: From abortion?

FATHER BENEDICT: Yes, from abortion. So we are dealing with the problem of evil. St. Thomas Aquinas said, very wisely, that the reason people — most people who believe — believe in God is because of the problem of evil, and the reason people — most people who don't believe — don't believe in Him is also because of the problem of evil. I probably know at least forty families who lost loved ones in the Towers, but . . . you do your best. You pick up the pieces. The mothers and the kids go on.

JOHN BISHOP: And there was a surge in faith, wasn't there?

FATHER BENEDICT: Oh, sure, for the moment.

JOHN BISHOP: Father, staying with the problem of evil, the other night on TV here, there was a heart-gripping story of two lovely little girls about seven, Siamese twins, with two heads, one body. Why? What is that about?

FATHER BENEDICT: Obviously, it is an accident of nature. At times God intervenes. One of the most remarkable miracles ever recorded was recorded at Lourdes in the presence of a Nobel Prize winner in medicine, Dr. Alexis Carrel. He was later head of the Rockefeller Institute. He saw a very sick woman patient recover in one hour and he said, "I have seen the resurrection from the dead." A woman sick unto death came back to life. She wasn't quite dead, but she was very close. So why does God work a miracle only now and again? That is the problem of evil. For me it is the reason I believe.

JOHN BISHOP: Father, the story in the Gospel where one of the apostles says to Our Lord, "Rabbi, who sinned, this man or his parents, that he was born blind?" (John 9:2) You know, the old Jewish idea of the sins of the father being visited on the sons. It seems rather harsh, but Our Lord replies, "It was not that this man sinned, or his parents, but that the works of God might be made manifest in him" (John 9:3). Would that mean, "Be careful, because He can withhold as well as give"?

FATHER BENEDICT: Yes.

JOHN BISHOP: It concentrates the mind. So when we see those Siamese twins, is it our distanced love for their condition that is in some way of value to them? Is this good enough as a thought?

FATHER BENEDICT: Well, it is an approach. Evil is a mystery. Christianity has many mysteries — unfathomable, impenetrable — some will last forever: "The depth of the riches and wisdom and knowledge of God! How unsearchable are his judgments and how inscrutable his ways!" (Romans 11:33)

JOHN BISHOP: Is that a Psalm?

FATHER BENEDICT: That is St. Paul. There are the mysteries of life: the Trinity, the Incarnation. There is one which is unfathomable because it is the mystery of darkness; that is evil. I don't think the human mind can comprehend the problem of evil. It has haunted many people. It haunts our own time.

JOHN BISHOP: Father, can I ask you about Christ's declaration from the cross, "*Eloi, Eloi, lama sabachthani?*" ("My God, my God, why hast thou forsaken me?" [Matthew 27:46; Mark 15:34])? You know some atheists and agnostics point to this and say, "You see, he gave up at the last minute."

I prefer to believe that He is reminding us in His dying breath of the Psalm which begins, "My God, my God, why hast thou forsaken me," (Psalm 22:1) and ends in a paean of praise and blast of glory.

So, Father, is Our Lord maybe doing it both ways? Showing that in His humanity he too can feel helpless for a second, a mini-second, and at the same time, as a Rabbi, teaching us in his last breath, "It is all right. I am the promised one, the Messiah"?

FATHER BENEDICT: The great theologian Hans Urs von Balthasar, in his book *Mysterium Paschale*, one of the great theological books of the twentieth century, goes into this. Christ had to drink to the dregs of the human condition. The feeling of abandonment which God knows we often have felt. Well, in His humanity He had to feel that. But it is of course also that Psalm fulfilled.

JOHN BISHOP: That's amazing.

FATHER BENEDICT: Well, it is part of the mystery of how the divinity of Christ fits with His humanity. May I say, though, somewhat ironically, those very people who object to that statement probably wouldn't say that he said anything else in the New Testament anyway?

JOHN BISHOP: They are being selective!

FATHER BENEDICT: Selective, yes. It is the only statement that they are going to take literally.

ATHEISM

———

JOHN BISHOP: Atheism, Father. I think it was Pope Paul VI who called for an apostolate against atheism during his pontificate. But I don't see anything happening, really. Everywhere you go, at least in the West, there is a presumption that there is no God. That is the bottom line, really.

FATHER BENEDICT: Not in the United States. Ninety-four percent of the people in the United States believe.

JOHN BISHOP: Oh, yes. I am talking from the British angle. The media, anyway, and academe have certainly made up their mind there is nothing. Atheism is the ruling philosophy.

FATHER BENEDICT: I don't know if even in England it's . . . I haven't worked that much in England.

The other day I had a very odd experience presiding at a Jewish funeral. I had a friend who was a non-religious Jew. A very fine man, an excellent man, but he had been raised without any Jewish commitment. He had worked all his life in civil rights for the government. So we had the funeral in a little Methodist chapel, and a number of blacks came who were very religious, a few Catholics, and an assortment of Jews, from religious Jews to secular Jews.

The service consisted of a number of people who got up and gave a little appreciation, and they wanted me to round it all off with a little statement or something. Only one or two people made no allusion to eternal life, and one of those who did not make an allusion to eternal life apologized to me later.

He said, "You see, I was raised without a religion." In fact, he was once one of my professors. He said, "My father was an atheist. So I really don't know what to say." Thus he apologized. But the rest of those supposedly secular, non-believing Jews were talking about their father or their brother being in eternal life. I don't take atheism very seriously.

JOHN BISHOP: Have you never had dark nights of unbelief?

FATHER BENEDICT: No. If I have dark nights, it would be anger at God.[5] But I love to talk to atheists. They are so nice because they work at it, you know. They say things like, "This is the only show you are going to have," or, "This is not a dress rehearsal." They make very good friends, except when they get old. They get bitter.

JOHN BISHOP: They don't have anyone to pray to, do they?

FATHER BENEDICT: No. You know, St. Anselm, using his ontological argument, would say that there must be a part of you — your will, your desire — to believe. You can't just do it in abstraction. Anselm would be following St. Augustine in that real belief is more than philosophical opinion. It calls to the whole being. It is a gift of God.

See, I am not a Thomist. I love St. Thomas Aquinas, but I am absolutely an Augustinian, Bonaventurian, Anselmian follower. And because I am a psychologist too, I don't think anyone ever changed for an idea. They had to have an investment in it. They have to have a desire. They have to want it. I mean, what would you do with the mere philosophical conviction that there is a divine being? Aristotle maintained that

God could not even know us because He is infinite. Plato was rather different. Plato prayed to God.

JOHN BISHOP: Yes, isn't that interesting? At the end of *The Republic*, there is a rather beautiful stanza in which he says something like, "Despite all our striving and writing and pondering, we have in the end to give it up to God."[6]

FATHER BENEDICT: Oh yes. As a Greek, Plato was a polytheist, but as a philosopher he was, at the end, a believer. Plato says, "In this world a person could build a raft with the ideas of wise men to take him across the river of death, but they would never know it was true unless someone came to reveal it to them, like God," which is almost a prophecy. Agnosticism annoys me a bit; but, you see, atheism is a belief. You see, if you are sure that there is no God, then you are a believer. You make an act of faith: "No God!"

JOHN BISHOP: That's right. The unbeliever's whole life can be structured on that belief.

FATHER BENEDICT: You see, you can't go and punch a hole in the sky and say, "There He is," or say, "There He isn't." You see, to me the existence of God, the presence of God, is so real — and it has been since I was a child — that it is impossible to deny.

CLERGY AND SEX

JOHN BISHOP: Father, what have you missed? No wife and family? What are the things you have missed because of your vocation?

FATHER BENEDICT: Well, I often say to the brothers it is perfectly obvious that whatever we missed, it wasn't the secret of happiness. I don't know an awful lot of our people who are terribly unhappy. I mean, if you came to see us you would be struck by the fact that we are extremely happy; almost raucously happy.

JOHN BISHOP: Of course I threw in that question because of the sex-abuse scandals at present confronting the Church. An argument is being put forward that suggests the Catholic Church should make an effort to get its priesthood married. The argument is that because the priests are sexually frustrated, they are attacking young boys, and so married clergy would be the cure.

FATHER BENEDICT: There is a very fine book called *Priests and Pedophiles*, by Dr. Philip Jenkins, a Professor at Penn State. He is not a Catholic. He says there is absolutely no evidence that sexual involvement with teenagers is more prevalent among celibate clergy than it is with other kinds of clergy.

A few months ago there were seventy-nine clergy in the United States up for abuse of minors. Forty-nine of them were Protestant ministers. The problem exists in the Orthodox Churches, where some priests are married. Sometimes it concerns girls rather than boys. But why did this happen? Because we did not teach the Ten Commandments.

JOHN BISHOP: When you say "we," who do you mean?

FATHER BENEDICT: Religious educators and teachers. We did not teach the last judgment. We did not teach mortal sin. We didn't deny these things, but we didn't teach them.

JOHN BISHOP: Well, yes, in our own family we have some lovely devout people and one of them has got the idea, because she doesn't read any theology, from some errant priest that, "If there is a hell, there is no one in it." She has the idea that everyone gets to heaven because all are forgiven at the last moment. This in the face of Our Lord's clear warnings about the danger of hellfire into which unrepentant souls will be thrust. How did this kind of erroneous teaching get into the corral, Father?

FATHER BENEDICT: I suspect it got in there by client-centered psychology. You know, don't blame all of psychology on Freud, Adler, Jung, Rogers, etc. They have all gone over Niagara Falls. They are completely passé in psychological circles.

I tell you, if you don't believe in the last judgment, go to Auschwitz, go to Dachau. You'll believe in the last judgment. Now, do I think many people go to hell? I hope not. I am somebody of the first hour. I knew I was going to be a priest when I was seven. I know the day, the minute, the moment when it came to me. I never thought of being anything else.

FATHER BENEDICT'S VOCATION

JOHN BISHOP: How did that vocation come to you, Father?

FATHER BENEDICT: Well, there was a very wonderful nun who taught us in the second grade: Sister Teresa. She was always patient and kind, and every day after school she would leave the convent and go down to a very poor neighborhood with a box or tray out of which would come steam on a cold day. I followed her. I was only in the second grade.

JOHN BISHOP: Was this in New York City?

FATHER BENEDICT: No; Jersey City. Have you been to Jersey City?

JOHN BISHOP: Well, we have been to New Jersey.

FATHER BENEDICT: No, I am talking about Jersey City. They have some tough people there; fascinating people. It is right across from New York City. I went to school there, looking at the Statue of Liberty from the back. Now there was a motion picture at the time, you may have seen it, *Snow White and the Seven Dwarfs*. There was a witch in it.

JOHN BISHOP: Oh yes, a great movie. Disney. What a scary witch!

FATHER BENEDICT: Well, where the sister went, there was a barber shop on the bottom floor of the tenement. The next time I got my hair cut there, I said to the old barber, Guiseppe, "What does the sister do who comes here every day?"

He said, "She's a taka care of de olda lady."

I said, "Why?"

He said, "She's a very sick."

I said, "Where does she live?"

"On a de topa floor."

So I went around to the back of the building. Now in Jersey City we have an architectural embellishment which does not exist anyplace else in the world. It is the wooden fire escape. It burns first! [*Much laughter*] So I climbed up.

On the second floor, I had to move through the tomato plants in cans — an Italian family. Third floor, beer bottles — the Irish. I got to the top floor and crawled over the milk delivery boxes, and I looked into the window and right there, three inches from my face, was the "wicked witch."

JOHN BISHOP: Good Lord!

FATHER BENEDICT: The "wicked witch." I can still feel the fright! I jumped over the milk boxes, knocked over the tomato plants, ran through the beer bottles, up the street, into the church, and threw myself in front of the statue of Our Blessed Mother, and I prayed. I asked, "How come the witch doesn't kill Sister Teresa?" Then I said to myself, "Maybe it is because Sister is nice to her. And if people were nicer to witches, maybe they wouldn't be so bad."

So that was the beginning. I never thought of being anything else but a priest.

In the seventh grade I read a poem by the great American poet Longfellow. It goes:

> In his chamber all alone,
> Kneeling on the floor of stone,
> Prayed the Monk in deep contrition
> For his sins of indecision,
> Prayed for greater self-denial
> In temptation and in trial;
> It was noonday by the dial,
> And the Monk was all alone.
>
> Suddenly, as if it lightened,
> An unwonted splendor brightened
> All within him and without him
> In that narrow cell of stone;
> And he saw the Blessed Vision
> Of our Lord, with light Elysian
> Like a vesture wrapped about Him,
> Like a garment round Him thrown.
>
> Not as crucified and slain,
> Not in agonies of pain,
> Not with bleeding hands and feet,
> Did the Monk his Master see;
> But as in the village street,
> In the house or harvest-field,
> Halt and lame and blind He healed,
> When He walked in Galilee.
>
> In an attitude imploring,
> Hands upon his bosom crossed,
> Wondering, worshipping, adoring,

Knelt the Monk in rapture lost.
Lord, he thought, in heaven that reignest,
Who am I, that thus thou deignest
To reveal thyself to me?
Who am I, that from the centre
Of thy glory thou shouldst enter
This poor cell, my guest to be?

Then amid his exaltation,
Loud the convent bell appalling,
From its belfry calling, calling,
Rang through court and corridor
With persistent iteration
He had never heard before.
It was now the appointed hour
When alike in shine or shower,
Winter's cold or summer's heat,
To the convent portals came
All the blind and halt and lame,
All the beggars of the street,
For their daily dole of food
Dealt them by the brotherhood;
And their almoner was he
Who upon his bended knee,
Rapt in silent ecstasy
Of divinest self-surrender,
Saw the Vision and the Splendor.

Deep distress and hesitation
Mingled with his adoration;
Should he go, or should he stay?
Should he leave the poor to wait
Hungry at the convent gate,

Till the vision passed away?
Should he slight his radiant guest,
Slight this visitant celestial,
For a crowd of ragged, bestial
Beggars at the convent gate?
Would the Vision there remain?
Would the Vision come again?
Then a voice within his breast
Whispered, audible and clear,
As if to the outward ear:
"Do thy duty; that is best;
Leave unto thy Lord the rest!"

Straightway to his feet he started,
And with longing look intent
On the Blessed Vision bent,
Slowly from his cell departed,
Slowly on his errand went.

At the gate the poor were waiting,
Looking through the iron grating,
With that terror in the eye
That is only seen in those
Who amid their wants and woes
Hear the sound of doors that close,
And of feet that pass them by;
Grown familiar with disfavor.
Grown familiar with the savor
Of the bread by which men die!
But today, they know not why,
Like the gate of Paradise
Seemed the convent gate to rise,
Like a sacrament divine

Seemed to them the bread and wine.
In his heart the Monk was praying,
Thinking of the homeless poor,
What they suffer and endure;
What we see not, what we see;
And the inward voice was saying:

"Whatsoever thing thou doest
To the least of mine and lowest,
That thou doest unto me!"

Unto me! but had the Vision
Come to him in beggar's clothing,
Come a mendicant imploring,
Would he then have knelt adoring,
Or have listened with derision,
And have turned away with loathing?

Thus his conscience put the question,
Full of troublesome suggestion,
As at length, with hurried pace,
Towards his cell he turned his face,
And beheld the convent bright
With a supernatural light,
Like a luminous cloud expanding
Over floor and wall and ceiling.

But he paused with awe-struck feeling
At the threshold of his door,
For the Vision still was standing
As he left it there before,
When the convent bell appalling,
From its belfry calling, calling,

Summoned him to feed the poor.
Through the long hour intervening
It had waited his return,
And he felt his bosom burn,
Comprehending all the meaning,
When the Blessed Vision said,
"Hadst thou stayed, I must have fled!"

JOHN BISHOP: Father, that was marvelous. Longfellow, eh?

FATHER BENEDICT: Yes, "The Legend Beautiful," by Henry Wadsworth Longfellow.

JOHN BISHOP: So what was the story behind Longfellow? He was not a Catholic.

FATHER BENEDICT: No. He was a Unitarian originally, but his dear wife burned to death in his presence. She caught fire in the fireplace and he was badly burned trying to put out the flames.

After that, he became quite Protestant and wrote poems about Luther and Calvin. But towards the end of his life, although he didn't become a Catholic, he wrote Catholic poems — like "Evangeline: A Tale of Acadia," about the expulsion of the French Catholics from Acadia by the British crown.

THE POOR

JOHN BISHOP: Father, it is obvious how committed you are to the poor. Let's examine your work with the poor and ask the deliberately ingenuous question, "Who are the poor and why are they there?"

FATHER BENEDICT: Well, in any society two or three, perhaps four percent of the people are not going to be able to take care of themselves. They are severely, emotionally disturbed. They are mentally ill, or they have been so traumatized by terrible experiences in childhood that they can't really function. Many of them have severe neurological difficulties. So that's the very poor. And every society has to take care of them.

Then you have the poor who can be helped, who are a social problem. Those disadvantaged, in this country for example, by slavery. Slavery did terrible damage. Then there are those who emigrated from very poor countries. Now they have to be helped to rise. You don't put them on the dole. The dole is absolutely "bread and circuses."

JOHN BISHOP: Oh, yes, the British know that from the bitter experience of the abused welfare services.

FATHER BENEDICT: We don't do that in this country.

JOHN BISHOP: The government in Britain is now trying to wean people off that system.

FATHER BENEDICT: Well they should. Now in New York we have "workfare." If you are on welfare benefits, you have to show up every day for eight hours and rake junk off the highways and sweep the streets. And you know, after about three months of that, some of them say, "I can make more money working," so they get a job.

You see, until now the kids had never seen an alternative before. Their parents were on the dole. They didn't know what it meant to work. In the sixties, President Lyndon Johnson and his government, with the "Great Society" scheme, didn't know how to distinguish between the very poor and the poor. We work with both, but we try to get the balance right. I have just paid 50,000 dollars for tuition for poor children in Catholic schools.

JOHN BISHOP: The money comes from public appeal?

FATHER BENEDICT: Sure. Last year we spent a million and a half dollars on the poor, and we gave out 250,000 pounds of food. We give it to the poor. We know the poor. Working with the poor is delightful. It is the happiest job you could have. Tonight, as we sit here talking, at 9:00 in our Padre Pio shelter they began the Rosary.

JOHN BISHOP: Where is that?

FATHER BENEDICT: In the South Bronx. It's a night shelter for twenty men off the street. Some of the men come in, you know, they might be black, Protestant, whatever; and they'll be saying the Rosary, and right in the middle of it someone will shout out, "Listen, Blessed Mother, you gotta come down and help me. Give us a break, Mother." They are praying out loud to the Blessed Mother!

JOHN BISHOP: Be careful, Father, say I with deep irony and more than a dash of sarcasm. You will be accused of the great crime of proselytizing!

FATHER BENEDICT: Oh, no, we don't. We get along very well with the simple evangelical black Protestants. It really is not Protestantism. It is black Christianity. It was given to them by the slave masters, but the black people developed their own and it is quite beautiful, and it doesn't have any heresy in it. We get along marvelously. Black people in the United States are not prejudiced against Catholics.

At our place in Harlem, the minister next door, she is a lady minister, presides over the Gates of Pearl Baptist Church. It is an old tenement, and the front of it is covered in pearl Formica. We have a wonderful time. St. Vincent de Paul says, "Love the poor and your life will be filled with sunlight and you will not be frightened of the hour of death."

JOHN BISHOP: My marvelous eighty-nine-year-old mother-in-law always says, "Never refuse a poor person. He might be Our Lord in disguise."

FATHER BENEDICT: Oh, it is Our Lord in disguise. Many of the poor we work with climb up the ladder.

JOHN BISHOP: Oh, that's good. You see success stories?

FATHER BENEDICT: Oh, lots, lots.

JOHN BISHOP: What about the house you have for unmarried mothers?

FATHER BENEDICT: We are part of a program called Good Counsel Homes. We have six houses for unwed mothers with babies, who don't want to have abortions, mostly girls off the street. We have one house for the mentally ill. The poorest person in America is a little baby who doesn't know that his mother is mentally ill and is dying of AIDS. We have that house right here in Westchester.

MOTHER TERESA OF CALCUTTA

JOHN BISHOP: Now, Father, you started all of this, didn't you?

FATHER BENEDICT: No, I was just part of the start.

JOHN BISHOP: No, but I mean the organization of it all.

FATHER BENEDICT: No plans. I got that from St. Vincent de Paul. No plans. Do what is in front of you to do, and if it expands, then fine.

JOHN BISHOP: That was echoed by Mother Teresa of Calcutta.

FATHER BENEDICT: Yes we also got that from Mother Teresa. No plans; be led. If you have plans, you are going to be confused into thinking God wants the plans.

JOHN BISHOP: I know you were very close to Mother Teresa. What about the attacks on her during her lifetime? Comments?

FATHER BENEDICT: Diabolical. You know there are some people who give sin a bad name! They really do.

JOHN BISHOP: She was said to have been manipulative. I'm trying to think of the better things said about her . . . too much missionary zeal . . .

FATHER BENEDICT: Did that man ever meet Mother?

JOHN BISHOP: We are talking about the writer Christopher Hitchens, aren't we? Yes, he said he met her in Calcutta. He was appalled at the state of her facilities.

FATHER BENEDICT: The state of her facilities? They weren't European. People made the same complaint about Albert Schweitzer. I was there. The premises were immaculately clean. I gave Mother and her sisters a Retreat. The mission was set up without assistance from the government.

At the time of Mother Teresa's death, the Missionaries of Charity were fully responsible for the total care of 50,000 destitutes. When I was there she had a huge place for physically handicapped children. We have two houses for AIDS patients.

I would love to take Hitchens on in a debate, but only if it was "live." I wouldn't take part in a canned debate.

Let me tell you, when we started the Friars of the Renewal we had 800 dollars and eight men. I met up with Mother Teresa — she was not part of the plan — and I said, "Mother you had better pray for me. I've got eight guys and 800 dollars."

She said, "Don't worry. God has lots of money!"

JOHN BISHOP: She is on her way to sainthood now, of course. How well did you know her, Father?

FATHER BENEDICT: I knew her for thirty-two years, and I was a witness for three hours at her beatification. I could take on some of the objections.

JOHN BISHOP: What were they?

FATHER BENEDICT: Well, probably the most serious objection was one that St. Francis had had leveled against him. She assumed that other people could do what she did. So if someone was feeling sick, she would say, "Well, just offer it up to Jesus." They couldn't do that. They were not that strong. So saints, I can tell you, often overestimate the strength of others.

I remember one day she was annoyed at me. She had asked me to do something, and I did it to the best of my ability. So she was nicely annoyed at me. But she was a very Victorian lady. She would scold you gently. I was in the car driving her and some of her sisters in the U.S.A. at one time, and she was giving me the needle piously. Being given the needle by Mother Teresa is like being harpooned by Captain Ahab! Anyway, we got to the convent, and it was midnight. I said to her, "Mother Teresa, can I speak to you for a minute? I am going to ask Cardinal Cooke to get someone else to be liaison. I am not angry, but this is just too much."

She said, "Sit down. Why do you think God chose you to be a priest?"

I said, "Mother, it is midnight."

She said, "Never mind."

I said, "I don't know why. I suppose it is because He has a sense of humor."

She said, "God chooses us because He is very humble. He chooses the weakest, the poorest, the most inadequate, to do His work." Then she said something very revealing. She said, "I pray that when I die the most unattractive, the most ungifted, of the sisters will take my place, and then everyone will know that this was not my work, but God's work." She looked me straight in the eye and she said, "Don't forget you were chosen by the humility of God." So that was it.

But, you know, she had a sense of humor. I was delegated to talking her into taking over the Carmelite convent in the South Bronx for her sisters. Now it was a nice place, it was a Carmelite convent, but it wasn't the Hilton. So we get out of the car and she goes, "Acha."

I said, "What's the matter?"

Now the building was not pretentious, but it was a little bit impressive. She says "The poor people will be afraid to come here."

I said, "Not the New York poor, Mother. They won't be one bit scared, I can tell you!"

So I took her to see Cardinal Cooke. Here I am between two saints. Cardinal Cooke's cause is up for beatification. Cardinal Cooke could charm the birds out of a tree. His parents came from Galway. He loved Mother Teresa. He was gentle and kind and a perfect gentleman. He started to charm Mother, and all of a sudden she says, "Your Eminence, help me. I am just a poor, weak old woman. Don't let me destroy the poverty of my order."

I could hardly keep a straight face. "Poor, weak old woman!" This is the one who a former Secretary General of the United Nations said was the most powerful woman in the world. Anyway, she didn't take the convent. The Cardinal said, "You know, Benedict, I could have twisted her arm."

I said, "You could have, and she would have had you on the floor in a half nelson!"

She said to me later, "What do you think about the whole thing?"

I said, "Well, Mother, to be honest with you, I was a bit humiliated, but not humbled, unfortunately. I am often humiliated but not humbled."

"Cheer up," she said, "humiliation could be a road to humility." [*Laughter*]

JOHN BISHOP: Father [*chuckling*], she was playing with you!

FATHER BENEDICT: Ah, yes. But do you know about the spiritual darkness she went through? Forty-five years of it.

JOHN BISHOP: No, tell us about it.

FATHER BENEDICT: It is a darkness that is thrust upon certain very gifted souls so that they will grow. If you have a sword and you want to strengthen it you put it in the fire.

JOHN BISHOP: When did it start for her?

FATHER BENEDICT: Right at the beginning of her ministry. It was mysterious. About eight weeks before she died, the day before she went back to India, I went down to see her and say Mass for her. Now there was always something somber about Mother, but on this occasion there she was on a cot. She couldn't stand at this stage; she was on her cot in the corner of the chapel. She was like an ice-cold, newly-opened bottle of champagne. Now imagine Mother Teresa like a bottle of champagne. She was bubbling. She was a little bit forgetful. She told me the same thing twice. But she was a different person, filled with joy, and she was telling me that she had 565 convents around the world, and she was bubbling away. I said to one of my confreres, Father Andrew Apostoli, later, "We will never see her again. She is going through the gates of paradise." St. Bonaventure speaks about that. The darkness had left her before she died.[7]

JOHN BISHOP: Father, was God being cruel to her?

FATHER BENEDICT: No, no, it was necessary. I think Mother Teresa is a world-class saint; a millennium star. If we manage not to blow up this stupid planet of ours, and people are still around in A.D. 3000, they will remember Mother Teresa of Calcutta.

JOHN PAUL THE GREAT

JOHN BISHOP: Father, are we living in an age of one of the great popes?

FATHER BENEDICT: It is my impression, although it may just be the enthusiasm of the moment; I think Pope John Paul II is the greatest pope since Innocent III.

JOHN BISHOP: Really? That goes back quite a bit.

FATHER BENEDICT: Yes, it does; to the time of St. Francis. I think he will be called John Paul the Great.

You know, there are three popes who have that encomium: Gregory the Great, Leo the Great, and Nicholas the Great. Nicholas the Great is not well known. But they have that title because they are popes who profoundly affected world history.

Leo sent Attila the Hun back. Gregory really took over the running of the western empire. Nicholas picked things up during the Dark Ages, when it all fell apart. The Carolingian dynasty didn't make it, and so Nicholas kept the post office open, so to speak.

I think Pope John Paul II has been marvelous. There are places where I think he has unfortunately failed. We all fail, but I think he failed particularly in the appointment of bishops.

JOHN BISHOP: Yes.

FATHER BENEDICT: I don't think he paid much attention to the minutiae of the daily running of the Church. You know, there was a writer, Schumacher.[8] Schumacher said that if the popes did not engage the new world that was emerging, the single globe, then the Church would become irrelevant.

I am sure the pope never read Schumacher, and when I read him years ago I thought, "Who is this guy, to tell the pope what to do?" But indeed that is what this pope did. He is a world-class presence. He is indeed a shepherd for the world.

As I said, I don't think he has done as well with the appointment of bishops as he might have done, but that depends on apostolic delegates. I think it shows an area where the government of the Church needs to be revised. I think we need to have primates.

JOHN BISHOP: Yes. The trouble is, this pope issues some marvelous statements and instructions, but bishops don't seem to obey him.

FATHER BENEDICT: Well, that has been happening since the "Sermon on the Mount." I mean, please. Read the New Testament. The apostles often didn't do terribly well with all their squabbling. Peter ran out. Please. I mean, did we ever have a worse day than Good Friday!

JOHN BISHOP: When the apostles all but deserted Him, you mean?

FATHER BENEDICT: Yes. Look, I am a disciple of St. Augustine. I don't expect much, so I don't get disappointed. It is a fallen world. The primary effects of original sin, which are the deprivation of grace and the loss of eternal life, are taken away by baptism or baptism of desire, but the other effects are not. These are the darkening of the intelligence, the weakening of the will, the casting of the emotions into chaos, and the corruption of human relationships. As far as I'm concerned, they seem to be continuing quite predictably and rather well at this time in our history! Look, I am not a Utopian; I am a New Yorker, and we think Utopia is a place in Queens! [*Laughter*]

FUTURE PLANS

JOHN BISHOP: Well, finally, there is always a finally, Father, what have you left undone that you want to do?

FATHER BENEDICT: Oh, I have no plans. Sufficient for the day. I would like to get my book on the history of devotions finished. It is about devotion to Christ — Catholic, Orthodox, and Protestant. I would have been afraid to die a few years ago because the community was new, but they are quite capable of going on without me, and doing much better, actually. So, *in manus tuas, Domine* (into your hands, Lord).

But there is one thing I would like to have, and that is a nice terminal illness — rather than have a heart attack or something like that. I would like to go out first-class! I want to do that so that I can make my final TV program which you can pick up for seven dollars and ninety-five cents and bring to a dying person.

JOHN BISHOP: What a great idea!

FATHER BENEDICT: You know, people are dying all the time, and nobody ever talks to them.

JOHN BISHOP: That would be an effective ministry to the dying.

FATHER BENEDICT: Yes. The American Medical Association did a study. Ninety-five percent of the people who are dying know they are dying and ninety-five percent of that ninety-five percent said that nobody ever spoke to them about dying.

So call it *Going First Class, How to Die Well.* You know, with a smile on your face and a song on your lips, and waving good-bye to them all.

JOHN BISHOP: Well, Father, I hope that video will be a long time in coming.

FATHER BENEDICT: Well, it is up to God, but I would like to get that done, and I also want to leave some remarks for my funeral on audiotape. My provincial, Father Ignatius, left a five-minute message on audiotape which was played at the end of his funeral Mass.

JOHN BISHOP: What did he say?

FATHER BENEDICT: Well, he wanted to thank us all for coming to his funeral! [*Much laughter*] You know, he is in the box and you hear the voice! Then he thanked God and his parents and the Catholic Church for the faith and the order, but he didn't thank the province of which he had been provincial. He fired a shot off the bridge!

When Cardinal O'Connor died, Cardinal Law was preaching and he said, "Cardinal O'Connor was always, all of his life, absolutely committed, as the Catholic Church is, to pro-life and the protection of the unborn."

Now President Clinton and Mrs. Clinton were in the front row and one of our brothers, a big teddy bear of a guy, gets up and begins to clap, and the whole place gets up and they clap for four minutes. So Clinton stood up, but he didn't clap! When I was walking out of the church, I met Al Sharpton. I said, "Al, what do you say?"

He growled, "He got in the last word!" [*Laughter*] It's a great line.

JOHN BISHOP: That had better be the last line. Thank you very much, Father.

FATHER BENEDICT: My pleasure.

NOTES FOR PART ONE

1. See the video *Crisis in the Church* (EWTN, 2002) and the book *From Scandal to Hope* (Our Sunday Visitor, 2002).

2. Alexander VI was pope from 1492–1503. Originally named Rodrigo Borgia, he became one of the most infamous of all popes through his neglect of the spiritual good of the Church.

3. George Weigel is a Catholic theologian and biographer of Pope John Paul II. An excerpt of his writings concerning the culture of dissent appears as an appendix in Father Benedict's book *From Scandal to Hope* (Our Sunday Visitor, 2002).

4. The sexual abuse scandals in the Catholic Church in America. See Father Benedict's book *From Scandal to Hope* (Our Sunday Visitor, 2002).

5. Father later explained that this refers to the thrashing around which we all experience from time to time when a loved one departs this life or a similar tragedy occurs.

6. The quote the interviewer is referring to reads, "But if you will listen to me, and believe that the soul is immortal and able to endure all evil and good, we shall always hold to the upper road, and in every way follow justice and wisdom" (Plato. *The Republic*. Everyman, 1992. Book 10, 621c, p. 320).

7. A privileged reading of some of Mother Teresa's correspondence to her spiritual directors shows her struggling with a great feeling of loss of God, of God not wanting her, of an inability from time to time to lift her soul to God. In the late 1950s, she wrote, "No light, no inspiration, enters my soul." But the darkness did not hinder her work and, as we know, she went on to glory.

8. Ernst Friedrich Schumacher. His book *Small is Beautiful: Economics As If People Mattered*, written in the 1960s, was a plea for "intermediate technology" to assist developing countries in facing up to the challenge of growth in the modern world.

PART TWO

Reflections after the Accident,
by Father Benedict Groeschel, C.F.R.

EDITOR'S INTRODUCTION TO FATHER BENEDICT'S REFLECTIONS

Father Benedict has preached from many pulpits throughout his priestly life, but perhaps never as eloquently as in the meditations he has delivered from his hospital bed over the past few months. On the following pages, Father shares his reflections on what has happened to him since his accident and where God is in the midst of it all. The messages are personal, yet applicable to every individual's life, because, as he says in his reflection on Good Friday, "It's everybody's feast day." Everyone suffers to some degree on any given day, but it is rare that someone preaches the Gospel in the midst of great suffering.

Saint Ignatius of Loyola once said, "If God causes you to suffer much, it is a sign He has great designs for you, and that He certainly intends to make you a saint." These words look nice in print, but they are a hard saying when the cross is imprinted upon your own flesh, as it has been for Father Benedict. It is not the mystical stigmata, like those Saint Francis or Saint Padre Pio were graced with, but a physical stigmata — a sharing in the cross of Christ that is both real and painful.

I remember Father Benedict telling me once many years ago that the quickest way for a person to progress on the spiritual path was to suffer greatly. In the interview on the previous pages, which took place before his accident, he reiterated that thought when he spoke of how he would like to die. Thankfully, Father has been graced with the suffering, but has not been taken from us. As he recovers from his wounds, you and I can benefit from his wisdom on the following pages no matter what our current situation might be.

I am reminded of a young woman who suffered from the day of her birth until her death at the age of twenty-four: Virginia Cyr. She suffered from Cerebral Palsy, was abandoned by her mother at an early age, was sent to an orphanage, and was then moved from one institution to another. Writing about her earliest memories, she said, "When I was a baby, not even a day old, my loving Father in heaven tapped me on the shoulder and asked me if I'd like to do something special for Him. I was just bursting with enthusiasm, and in my timid, baby way, I accepted the challenge" (*Virginia Cyr: God's Little Hobo*, Our Sunday Visitor, 2004). For Virginia, a life of suffering and rejection was an acceptance of an invitation to carry the cross behind Jesus.

Just as Saint Paul wrote to the Galatians, "Henceforth let no man trouble me; for I bear on my body the marks of Jesus" (Galatians 6:17), so too Father Benedict's acceptance of suffering and his probing of the meaning of it all give all of us much to reflect upon. These reflections are perhaps best read one at a time, taking time to meditate on their import for how we live our own lives and how we deal with the interruption of our plans, our hopes, and our desires. As Father says, "There are no accidents." If we take that as a given and follow his advice, we too will be led to "trust God in all things."

MICHAEL DUBRUIEL

THE PROVIDENCE OF GOD

I am still in the hospital after my severe accident. On January 11, 2004, I was in Florida preparing to give a workshop to 125 priests when a car hit me at a busy intersection near the Orlando International Airport. I never expected such a thing to happen. I don't remember the next month, but they tell me that I came right to the door of death. For a moment, I had no heartbeat, pulse, or blood pressure; but I guess God didn't want me.

When I finally came around, and knew what was going on, I realized the tremendous reaction of support and prayer that my accident had caused. The first day after the accident, the Franciscan Friars of the Renewal website (www.franciscanfriars.com) had several thousand hits from people seeking information about my accident. I am so very, very grateful.

I want to thank you all for the hundreds of get-well cards; I want to thank you for your prayers, especially very fervent prayers; I want to thank friends of many different religious denominations who sent me e-mails. Each day I try to read some of them, although I cannot possibly read them all. But a member of our volunteer staff reads every one of them. Certain letters are selected for me to have an opportunity to read. I am extremely grateful to you!

We should always be grateful to God for whatever happens. I didn't foresee this accident happening. I have always preached that we must always trust God, even in the things that he only permits to happen. I guess God wanted me to prove the strength of my convictions. So, although I'm disappointed in being limited, I want to say that I completely trust in the Lord and in His providence.

THERE ARE NO ACCIDENTS

This is the first opportunity I have had to personally thank the people who have been caring for me since my accident. I was deeply moved by the amount of prayer, cards, and e-mails from many, many people. I don't know how to repay you for your expressions of support and letters of encouragement.

I am going to be laid up for a while, healing and hopefully getting stronger. I am thankful to God that I did not sustain any serious head injuries or facial disfigurement. God must be telling me to get back to work.

On March 10, 2004, I spoke for the first time in two months. I am so grateful for the brothers who have attended to my needs, especially Brother Daniel and Brother Peter. They have shown infinite patience to a person in a desperate situation. I can't tell you how happy I am to have been so well cared for by the staff of two very fine hospitals. I will be forever grateful to these generous people for the rest of my life. People say love and faith are dying away in this country, but here I see so much dedication and care — the attendants, nurses, specialists, and of course, the doctors.

I want to share with you two principles upon which I have built my life. The first is from St. Augustine: "God does not cause evil, but that evil should not become the worst." Second: "There are no accidents. Evil things occur because of bad will or stupidity or fatigue, yet whatever the cause God will bring good out of it if we let Him."

I had seen the movie *The Passion of the Christ* before I had my accident. How many times the haunting scenes (of Christ's agony) brought me consolation and hope when things were very dark.

WASTED PAIN

On March 10, I began to be able to speak again. This makes life easier, and in many ways, more enriching. Speech permits us to not be locked up in our little room of self.

When Father Luke, a young friar of our community, offered Mass, we welcomed someone from down the hall, Professor Alice von Hildebrand, a distinguished Catholic writer and the wife of the late Dietrich von Hildebrand. Alice and I have been close friends for many years and you may have seen our series on suffering on EWTN. She reminded me of a very important line which I had forgotten. It was a statement by Archbishop Fulton J. Sheen: "Nothing is worse than wasted suffering." Of course, one is tempted to ask, "Why did this accident occur?" While I am being tempted to ask this, I am looking at a picture of St. Padre Pio, who said, "Don't ask why, ask what — what am I supposed to do?" That seems rather obvious, except one must admit a deficiency of virtues and throw oneself before Christ crucified and the Holy Spirit.

We all suffer. Some suffer well, some poorly, some bitterly, some in union with Christ, some in union with Our Lady and the saints, some in union with God as they know Him, some only in union with the other people in the hospital, and some all alone — but we suffer. How much better it is to suffer even poorly and inconsistently in union with Christ.

GRATITUDE

When you are severely deprived of the common human experiences of eating and drinking, of walking and talking, you can do one of two things: you can count your blessings and enjoy them; or you can slip into a dangerous depression which might severely jeopardize your recovery. What is there to be thankful for? There is a whole list of things! You could be thankful that you are alive. I know this because, as the physicians were working many strenuous hours to bring me back, Father John Lynch, who had accompanied me to the hospital, beseeched them to keep going. At the end of a few minutes, I was a barely functioning human being; but I was alive!

People have asked me if I had one of those life-after-death experiences. I can honestly say, "no," but there is no doubt that, medically speaking, I walked in the shadow of death. It makes life very precious — all sorts of things start to fall into a profound perspective: pro-life, euthanasia, even the general question of how we treat those who are needy or incapacitated.

THE PASSION OF CHRIST

One of the most significant things about being sick in the hospital is the meaning of pain. We should not seek pain as a good in itself, although sometimes Christians are mistakenly prone to do this.

Pain is basically an alarm system in which our body lets us know that something is wrong. When there are many injuries which are sustained, some pain will honestly feel like the worst you've ever endured. Other pain will be persistent, low level, and just annoying.

If you saw *The Passion of the Christ* recently, you can realize the immense variety of pain, some of it unendurable. Many times in the past months I have thought of scenes from *The Passion of the Christ*, which I was privileged to see before it was released. When you think of Christ's pain — His motive for enduring it, His generosity in redeeming our sins, the incredible fact that He even survived to get to Calvary, and the rather clear descriptions we are given by the Evangelists — then, although we do not look for pain, we have reason enough to accept it and to entrust its mysterious presence in our lives to Jesus crucified. We also have reason to reach out more patiently and more consistently to those who suffer. Let us continue to pray for one another!

OUR DEPENDENCY ON CHRIST

When one is in the hospital for a long period of time, especially with limited ability to move and no ability to speak, it is very easy to move into the great library of your own thoughts. It is there that you meet God and there that you evaluate the world around you. It becomes very clear that life, reduced to its simplest dimensions, is a purgatory; the whole world reduces in importance to being able to grab the call bell or to get a glass of water. You might recall that when you are in a hospital and are unable to speak, you are also unable to eat or drink. Our Lord's frequent use of the idea of water and grace has all the more meaning when you haven't had a glass of water in two months.

In such situations, it is very easy — perhaps almost inevitable — to become a bit infantile. Brother Daniel, Brother Peter, and Dave Burns can tell you all about it. Meditating about it makes it all clear that our apparent spiritual growth is rather fragile. As I looked back on my life, the prayer that became a rock inside of my being was "Lamb of God who takes away the sins of the world, have mercy on us." We have always been lambs of God, completely dependent on Christ for everything; but we easily forget this, and seldom see our complete spiritual dependency on Christ except at times of great need.

"I AM WITH YOU!"

The experience of being hospitalized and debilitated gives us a tremendous opportunity to appreciate what others mean in our lives — most importantly our attentive relatives and friends. This is one of the great blessings of belonging to a vibrant, functioning religious community. The people at the hospital expressed to me their amazement at the concern of the brothers and sisters of our community. The presence of your immediate family is an invaluable gift at this time.

Among other gifts are the wonderful staff members and personnel you meet in the hospital. I have found that greeting them with a smile and expressed gratitude brought forth the most remarkable concern and kindness both in Florida and in New York. The kindness and care of literally dozens of health care workers will always remain in my memory. It is worth mentioning that the vast majority of these workers were not Anglos — they come from the Orient, China, the Philippines, Africa, the Caribbean, and South and Central America. Some were more recent arrivals from Europe. The willingness to do most unpleasant tasks and the kindness that brought them around at the end of the day to say "good night" with a cheerful smile was most encouraging. The care of physicians and technological staff is all the more impressive when one considers the burdens that they carry.

And finally there is the presence of God. In the several weeks of strong pain medication, it is hard to focus your mind; but you become aware that faith is not a human accomplishment, but rather a response to a gift. Through all the haze I recall a presence, sometimes like a person standing in the wind and rain saying, "Do not be afraid, I will be with you."

GOD STILL WANTS YOU HERE

If you have followed my preaching and writing over the years, you know that the most significant part of my application of the Gospel to everyday life has been the acceptance of God's will and divine providence. I've tried personally to live this out, but I had no idea that in my later years I would be confronted with so great a challenge as now faces me.

Apparently, by a medical miracle, I am still alive — having really been considered dead. One can't miss the conclusion that when this happens, God still wants you here. Consider how many times in the course of life we are in danger of death and not even aware of it!

I don't know what God has in store for me, nor do you know what He has in store for you; yet a conviction that must guide us both is "Your will be done." This conviction should be the ultimate intention of all of our prayers — along with finding our peace in the acceptance of that will. Certainly, to pray like this is a gift of the Holy Spirit.

PROGRESS

From what I'm told, I am making progress in my recovery; however, there are still big challenges ahead, such as learning to walk again and regaining full use of my right arm. If you've ever been in this position, you know that it is very encouraging to know how far you've come, yet very frightening to realize how far you still have to go. I'm sure some of you have had or will have a similar experience of sorrow and disaster. It seems to me that the spiritual answer is to be found in neither optimism nor pessimism about the future, but in complete trust in God. He sent us into this world to do certain things. We may not know His will for us; however, it will be fulfilled if we keep the commandments and take the opportunities for doing good that are set before us. It is out of two things, acceptance and obedience to God, that we receive the great gift of peace.

HOPE

In the daily rounds of life, one of the most important things that we hardly ever think about is hope. As St. Paul says, "In this hope we are saved" (Romans 8:24). He also says that we are saved by faith and charity. This strikes me in these long days in the hospital when inevitably I think of all the apostolic things I could be doing — and I get discouraged.

In my room I have pictures of several saints. Many of them fought illness and, humanly speaking, did not achieve their potential in life; however, the Lord has raised them up to tell us it is not important what you do but why you do it. Two of my special friends are St. Thérèse and St. Bernadette, both of whom struggled with great illness and died very young, having accomplished, from a secular point of view, practically nothing. Why should I complain with my limited talents? I got hit with disaster at seventy years old, and everybody around here keeps telling me I look great and am getting better.

In your life, when difficulty, even catastrophe occurs, remember hope. Not only the hope of God's help, but the hope of eternal life.

THANKSGIVING

One of the great realizations that come when a disaster wipes you out in a few minutes is how good and faithful people can be. Not only have the friars and sisters kept going; it's my realization that they have done better than if I were around putting in my two cents!

Several groups of lay people have also come to the rescue and continue to assist in the collection of alms, in the thanking of benefactors, and in the paying of bills. Beyond that, several apostolic endeavors that I felt inspired to start kept right on going. The St. Francis House never missed a beat. Yolanda and Jerry Cleffi visited me recently and gave me a marvelous report on the growth of the Oratory of Divine Love, a prayer movement for informed lay people.

It is wonderful to know that these works go on so beautifully — because it shows that they are works of the Holy Spirit. He is still running the world.

One of the beautiful experiences of my accident has been the dedication and helpfulness of close friends and confreres. I will never be able to adequately thank Brother Daniel and Brother Peter, who have provided the services of full-time practical nurses. David Burns and Father John Lynch were not only faithful at the time of the accident — which they almost witnessed — but have stuck by me ever since. The wonderful staff at Orlando Regional Medical Center literally kept me alive by their dedication. Volunteers like John Delgado went to great personal sacrifice to care for the friars and other visitors who came to see me in Florida. The staff at the hospital here in New York also provided wonderful care and moved me along. I am now in a new facility, and later on I will thank those who are presently helping me.

Generous benefactors have come to the aid of the friars and assisted with expenses not covered by insurance — and they still continue to help! Father Gene Fulton and the staff of Trinity Retreat have responded like family. I am ever grateful to all, literally tens of thousands of people, who took the trouble to send me a card or e-mail.

I guess the secret of why people have been so generous is to be found in the grace of God, in the gifts of the Holy Spirit, and in charity, which, as St. Paul says, pushes us on. God reward you all!

OFFERING IT UP!

For those of us who went to Catholic school in the old days, one of the most powerful spiritual messages that the sisters gave us was to unite our own pains and troubles with the Church. The famous phrase "offer it up" was an important part of the spirituality of devout Catholics and the students who, it was hoped, would become devout Catholics.

The idea was never quite clear; in fact, it was mysterious how our sufferings and pains would have anything to do with the sufferings of Christ for the salvation of the world. But nonetheless, like many mysteries, we believed it. As we grew older, the great text in Colossians 1:24 began to mean more to us: "I rejoice in my sufferings for your sake, and in my flesh I complete what is lacking in Christ's afflictions for the sake of his body, that is, the church." Therefore, those of us who still believe that you can "offer it up" have a great motive to try to put up with our sufferings. It would be wonderful if we could always do this bravely and with a smile, but that may not be realistic or necessary. The mere fact that we try, that we don't give up, that we go on in the darkness, is sufficient indication that we are trying to please God, and surely He must see it this way.

"THY WILL BE DONE"

When a calamity or distressing situation comes into our lives — such as an incurable illness, the birth of an incapacitated child, or an accident like the one I just experienced — faith and grace will help us to say, "Thy will be done" (Matthew 26:42).

It takes plenty of help from God, and our own willingness to believe, to do this, but we often don't recognize what is implied. It means that day after day one accepts the distressful results of the illness or incapacity. Day after day, a person with an incurable illness, an incapacitated loved one, or a chronic disease, lives out the details of the statement, "Thy will be done."

That is where God is truly honored: in the small details He brings about good from evil. This was a powerful message in *The Passion of the Christ*. In detail after detail, we saw Christ accepting one horror after another — all as part of His prayer, "Not my will, but thine, be done" (Luke 22:42).

DEALING WITH SETBACKS

During my recovery, I ended up taking a step backwards, returning to the hospital. I left the nursing home sadly.

For some reason, I have a case of anemia, and they can't figure out why. But, like everything else, we put it in the hands of God.

It's understandable that when trials occur, and finally seem to be coming to an end, we expect God to send blue skies everywhere. The trial is seen as an exception to life, and God has to right the exception.

Indeed, that's not the case. Trials can be long and unrelieved. I remember the very devout seminarian Eugene Hamilton (see his book *A Priest Forever*, Our Sunday Visitor, 1998) telling me of the disappointments and bad test results and setbacks, and how he clung to the cross of Christ in the midst of it all.

Our Lord was to lead Eugene to ordination in the hour of death, but he only got there because he trusted God bravely and prayerfully. When troubles come to us, the question is: "Do we wish to trust God, or do we choose to feel frustrated by the silly thought that He has forgotten us?"

KEEPING FAITH

One of the most important things to do in sickness, trouble, disaster, or hurt in our lives is to not lose heart. It would be wonderful if we never lost heart at all. But, as with most things in the spiritual life, "it ain't so simple."

To keep your trust and confidence, you must constantly be able to deal with disappointment — with a sense of free-falling into disaster and of looking into the distance and seeing the horrible monster called "loss of faith."

When things go badly, a phrase comes to me: "Keep the faith." I was talking to a wonderful young woman I've known all her life. She is in the last stages of ALS (Lou Gehrig's Disease), but can manage to talk to me with the technical miracle of a computer that operates from her eye. Unable to move, she wrote to me recently, "I keep my faith." This is what we all must do. It isn't a simple choice. It's like loving someone. You've got to go over and over it again. Most people have crises in their lives, and a great many people have disasters. In every life comes sorrow. A wonderful example to follow is Anne Morrow Lindbergh, who, as she writes about in her book *Hour of Gold, Hour of Lead* (Harvest Books, 1993), turned to the crucifix.

TIME TO REFLECT

Hospitals give you lots of time to think. They permit you to stand back from life and to look at the meaning of suffering, of error, and even of the wickedness of one person to another. At present we're likely to be in the hospital only a few days — perhaps a shorter time than we should be. The longer we stay, the more opportunity we have to think about life and its meaning. How sad it is to see people spend the whole time watching television and considering their own thoughts and positions.

It takes a real effort to stop and take stock of yourself, because in our society even religious people are not accustomed to doing this. All people, sick or well, would be very wise to build into their schedule a time to think about God, and to think about themselves in relationship to God, from Whom we come and to Whom we return.

HOSPITALS AND FAITH

One of the very best things about hospitals is that they bring together a lot of people who should be turning to God. Not just patients, but the staff. This may explain why, in the past, all hospitals had religious orientations and names. But even now, the amount of religious belief and fervor in the hospitals is quite amazing.

I have been in secular hospitals since my accident in January. I have found them to be at least even superficially religious. I've given out dozens of my books to staff members who were exceptionally kind — they all felt very blessed to receive them. The visits of the groups of our brothers and sisters were the object of much courtesy and positive talk.

The other night, six sister novices came to my room and sang traditional hymns such as "Jesu, Joy of Man's Desiring." Their presence in the hospital evoked a very positive reaction. Part of the reason is that people are not only looking to save life but also wonder what happens when life is over. A positive expression of faith reassures them that we are the creatures of a merciful God — something that many do not know.

REASON TO BE HAPPY

Being seriously incapacitated, even for a period of weeks or months, makes us aware of a tremendous number of blessings we often take for granted. The other day, with the help of three people, I managed to take a dozen steps. I was exhausted for an hour or two afterward.

How many hundreds of thousands of steps do we take in life and never give them a thought? Because of this, we neglect many opportunities to thank God. When the friars distribute food on holidays in the south Bronx, a dear little old black lady, Ruby Davis, always comes by. She is forever smiling, and one day I asked her, "Ruby, what are you so happy about?"

"I'm so grateful to God for all that I have," she answered. "I can see, I can hear, I can walk, and I can talk."

She's quite right to be grateful for those elementary functions. I spent two months unable to speak, and I still cannot walk. How thankful to God I will be when walking and other commonplace functions of life return to me through the mercy and generosity of God.

INSTRUMENTS OF GOD

Each day I see elderly and chronically ill people for whom life has little left to give. They go on for a variety of reasons, and a little examination will reveal that the reasons are more religious than they might at first appear to be. We live with the illusion that our country is almost totally secularized despite the fact that something like *The Passion of the Christ* reveals a great deal of religious sentiment. The reason is that God's grace does not depend entirely on our efforts; in fact, it depends very little on us. We are simply the witnesses of grace, and the clergy are simply the channels of sacramental grace. How narrow-minded we would be to think that God's grace is limited to our efforts.

Our Lord's life reveals that He was often accepted by sinners and people with little apparent religious conviction, like the woman at the well in John 4. We who are devout Christians should not be discouraged by the secularism we see all around us. Unseen and unknown, Christ is calling and the Holy Spirit is at work.

I received a letter recently from a Carmelite nun. In an earlier letter to her, I had remarked how difficult it must be to live in a cloister today when the environment everywhere is so secular. Sister wrote back, telling me of the warm reception and great interest their little Carmelite cloister had received from the people in their area. She said that although many had no knowledge of the Faith, they still felt called to pray and try to find a way to God.

We all need to learn that God does His work in us, and that we are simply His instruments. Believe me, after being in the hospital, I can say that our country is far more religious that it sometimes appears.

LIVE BY LOVE

Outside my little office at Trinity Retreat is a rough artificial stone with the printed words: "Do no great things, only small things with great love — Mother Teresa."

I put it there some time ago to remind myself that at times I have experienced success in apostolic work and some devout people have been kind enough to think I have done a few good things. Although I am not a founder, but only one of the founding friars of the Franciscan Friars of the Renewal, our community is making a noticeable contribution to the reform of religious life.

I remind myself very often that God does His best work with those whom the world thinks of as fools, that He does not need any one of us, and that the most productive life ever lived was cut off at thirty-three years by malice and jealousy. Now I realize, after months in the hospital, that I still overestimated the impact of my preaching. I've learned the hard way that God is still running the world and that Christ is still saving the world.

St. Catherine of Siena made a startling statement that I used to find overly severe. She said that the Lord revealed to her that she was nothing and that He was everything. Some of us learn the hard way. Our most important task is to live by love.

PENANCE

We all know that we need to be sorry for our sins, and yet we seem to know it much less than we used to. Personal penance, which in some way was painful or unpleasant, used to be part of the Christian life. For Catholics, it meant fasting, extra prayers, generosity to the poor, and just putting up with life without complaining.

Somehow, in the last few decades, we moved away from any unpleasantness in fulfilling our Christian duties. We felt we had to have cushy, padded kneelers in church. We now have practically no Eucharistic fast, and our current Lenten fast would have brought laughter to the early Christians or even to those of the early twentieth century. Penance is supposed to be tough. As the three sacred days of Holy Week approach, those of us in the hospital have little opportunity to do traditional penances. Because of illness, we also feel that we are doing enough. Perhaps a lot of other people who are not in the hospital but who have severe problems, heavy crosses, or chronic difficulties with family all feel that they too are doing enough. But this is a time to do more, or to do better what we always do, and to do it with much love for Christ.

Because of the film *The Passion of the Christ*, millions of people have a better awareness of what Christ suffered for us. Penance is the scriptural way of showing one's gratitude.

GOOD FRIDAY IN A HOSPITAL

A hospital, especially one dedicated to the care of people with chronic physical disabilities and particularly extreme old age, is a remarkable place to spend Good Friday.

"Behold the wood of the cross." All around you, people are experiencing their personal Calvary. But when you think of it, this is true in any neighborhood, any family, and any place where human beings gather. Even working in a business office, there are people going through their personal Calvary or, unfortunately, their personal hell. This is why the great message of Good Friday is charity. "God so loved the world that he gave his only Son" (John 3:16), and His Son brought us salvation and the hope of eternal life. Even the criminals and sadists who led Christ to Calvary were included in His prayer, "Father, forgive them..." (Luke 23:34).

In a very touching scene in *The Passion of the Christ*, Jesus, beaten and exhausted, meets Mary on the way to Calvary. The character of Jesus, borrowing from the Book of Revelation, says, "Behold, I make all things new" (Revelation 21:5). Some of the early Church Fathers tell us that among those gathered to receive the Holy Spirit at Pentecost were some who had shouted, "Crucify Him!" in Pilate's courtyard.

By faith, even those in very desperate situations can participate in the commemoration and reality of Good Friday. It's everybody's feast day.

CHRIST IS RISEN!

One of the truly great changes in the Church in the last fifty years has been the reform of the Easter Vigil liturgy. Incredibly, I recall as an altar boy arriving at church at 6:30 on Holy Saturday morning for the Easter Vigil. At that early hour, one solitary priest and the acolytes began the Easter Vigil and Mass, which would usually take place at record speed in the presence of several devout elderly women who never missed anything at church.

The goal of the interminably long Latin readings and the lighting of the new fire seemed to be the production of Easter water. This water was blessed in huge galvanized tubs, and as the liturgy came to an end at about 8:15, a curious spectacle would ensue. The church would begin to fill with all sorts of devout people carrying a vast assortment of bottles — milk bottles, blue milk-of-magnesia bottles, and other bottles that gave rise to the suspicion they may have once held alcoholic spirits. Later, when I served Mass at the Dominican mother-house, I remember another experience: a feeling of exultation as the sisters chanted the Gloria and the convent bells announced Christ's resurrection. Unfortunately, this was twenty-three hours before Easter morning.

The Easter Vigil, as it is now celebrated on the evening of Holy Saturday, with the new fire blazing dramatically in the church courtyard, cannot fail to fill faithful souls with something of the mystery and glory of Christ. This year, I will celebrate the Vigil alone, reading the liturgical prayers and looking forward to celebrating Mass with my fellow patients the next morning in the hospital.

Father Mariusz, from our community, will be principal celebrant, and I will be seated in a wheelchair with still broken bones and many other problems. I expect, however, to be just as happy that Christ is risen. And I can't complain, because I remember celebrating the Vigil once at the Church of the Holy Sepulchre in Jerusalem. After that liturgy, I knelt in the cave of the cross, and it meant so much that Christ is risen.

Being in the hospital, especially for a long time, reminds one that we are on a journey and that we have here no lasting home. Christ calls us to a world where there is no mourning or weeping or crying anymore. How happy we will be then that Christ is risen!

ASK, "WHAT AM I TO DO?"

Recently, I had visits with the two people who were with me on the evening of my accident on January 11, Dave Burns and Father John Lynch. Together we went over some of the events of that terrible evening and my very narrow escape from death.

I had been wondering about the things for which I could be thankful to God, and we began to list many things: I did not have a severe brain injury or a bad deformity of the face or mouth; I seem to be recovering even the use of my limbs; and the doctor told me he thinks I may be able to regain use of my elbow and, consequently, my right arm. All these things are blessings in a situation that may look like a terrible calamity.

It is always important to remind ourselves that God does not do evil, but that He keeps evil from becoming the worst. There are natural disasters like tornadoes; there are disasters such as wars, which are caused by human beings; and there are accidents where human beings in their functioning miscalculate or misdirect something. Why blame these things on God?

As I look back, I can see the many blessings I have received, and I do not really want to ask, "Why?" As Saint Padre Pio, a man I admire so much, used to say, "Ask rather, 'What am I to do? What can I do with the rest of my years or months?'"

The real Christian wants to do what God wants him to do. Perhaps the saint is the one who wants this to a perfect degree. The struggling sinner like me wants this only imperfectly. Thus, we have certain kinds of unhappiness which the saints do not have. But we'll get there someday.

WHAT GOD PERMITS

Why, you ask yourself (and so do I), is it so hard to accept what God permits, not what He causes?

If we think of the immense sorrow of the Blessed Virgin Mary, it is perfectly legitimate to ask why we didn't go from the Last Supper to the Ascension and miss all the terrible suffering in between. God knew what was going to happen; Christ knew what was going to happen. He shrank from the suffering that awaited Him and asked if God's will could be changed. That was His human nature.

In His human nature, even Christ appears not to be totally passive about what the Father wills. Therefore, it cannot be wrong to ask if some misfortune or cross that looms before us, or is already upon us, can be taken away. Christ Himself does it during His agony in the garden. Beyond that, however, we must be determined always to see our suffering through, to carry the cross all the way, no matter what.

THE MYSTERY OF THE CROSS

Why some of us have to endure great sufferings in life is an interesting question. Think of all the people in the twentieth century who died horribly in war — children, civilian populations, people in concentration camps. Why did that happen?

Many of these people firmly believed in God. Many prayed to God that there would be peace and that they would not be caught in the huge conflagration of war. And we don't have to go back the beginning of the twentieth century; we only have to look at recent military conflicts or uprisings in the Near East.

The answer is partly that God gives human beings freedom and does not run the world like a puppet show. Another reason is that it is in overcoming evil that good is ultimately accomplished. It seems to us that everything should be good and that evil should simply disappear. That sounds like a good idea, but it is not what happens.

So I sit here in the hospital with an evil — the right side of my body badly injured. It probably will lead to a shortening of my life, since I was an older person when I had this trauma.

But is that so evil? No. It seems to me that in following God and trusting in Him, or by turning to Him in dark hours, we can change evil into good. That is the mystery of the Cross.

VISITING THE SICK

When we run into difficult situations, we often find that family and friends come to our assistance, and that can be a most consoling thing. The brothers and sisters of my community, together with my own family and friends, have made my own difficult experience much more bearable. I will always be grateful to them.

There are, however, times when people are alone. As I look around the nursing home where I am recovering at the moment, I see so many elderly people and even those with illnesses in their late sixties and early seventies, who appear to be terribly alone. It seems so tragic.

Wouldn't it be wonderful if, in our society, it became a custom among Christians to visit one sick person or lonely person in a nursing home or hospital every week? It would turn Sunday morning after Mass into a time of great blessedness.

In my present situation, I am aware that there are so many good people who for one reason or another have no one to support them. Jesus says in the Gospel according to Matthew: "I was sick and you visited me, I was in prison and you came to me" (Matthew 25:36).

Putting this into action would be a good resolution to make.

DEATH IS NEVER FAR AWAY

One of the things you learn in the hospital is that death is not far away from any of us. Two people have died in the last week where I am staying. Although they were elderly, their passing brought sorrow and grief to their families. This might puzzle some in our culture, because the quality of their life was very poor, but it is explained by the fact that God has endowed us with an instinctive fear of death — and also by the fact that death is a parting.

For the person who does not believe, or who has a weak faith, it is a frightening reality; but for the Christian believer death is the entrance into life. In the past, even the funeral Mass concentrated on the sad and fearful aspects of death. Now, the liturgy more appropriately calls us to joyful hope and fervent prayer for our loved one who is gone.

My experience during the two months I was on a respirator and unable to speak, eat, or drink gave me a new view of purgatory. I used to joke about this reality — I will no longer joke about it, however, because in some ways I was there.

St. Thomas More, in his great prayer in the Tower of London while awaiting execution, prayed to "have ever before mine eyes my death which is ever at hand, to pray for pardon before the judge comes, and to have continually in mind the passion that Christ suffered for me." What we learn from the words of this great saint is how we must get ready and how we find the real meaning of life with its suffering and its hope.

CALL OF DIVINE MERCY

In some respects, a hospital brings out the best or the worst in people. People who are really ill, who have been hospitalized for a long time, or who are just having a difficult time with it all may regress and act childishly, and they may be very embarrassed when they do this. On the other hand, others will feel fairly "up" and present a stiff upper lip and a bold face. We sometimes see this when we visit a terminally ill patient who has accepted his condition and is at peace. It's quite remarkable.

Many people in the hospital, however, especially the elderly, just seem to fade slowly into the distance. They don't speak much, they have few interests, and they don't seem to come out of themselves. People get annoyed at this; perhaps I sometimes get annoyed at it myself, since I'm in a nursing home. But they are preparing to leave, to get on the boat.

I am so grateful that I believe in the God of infinite mercy. All around me I see people who don't look as if they are going, but who are in fact being called by God and summoned home. They may not even be consciously aware of this, but at a certain moment they will hear Christ call them. They will know the truth of the divine mercy revelation.

How You Can Help the Franciscan Friars of the Renewal

"Francis, the servant of God, returned to Saint Damian Church. He set to begging for the stones with which to restore the church. He called to passers-by: 'Whoever gives me one stone will have one reward; two stones, two rewards; three stones, a triple reward!'" (*The Three Companions*, 21).

"The brothers shall not acquire anything as their own, neither a house nor a place, not anything at all. Instead, as pilgrims and strangers in this world who serve the Lord in poverty and humility, let them go begging for alms with full trust" (*Rule of Saint Francis*).

Dear Friends,

As Franciscan Friars of the Renewal, we own no real estate and we do not receive any regular salary or stipend for our apostolic preaching or work with the poor. Rather, in "a humble spirit of dependence on Divine Providence" (C.F.R. Constitutions), we rely upon the offerings of friends, family members, relatives, and benefactors to sustain our way of life. Although we try to live as frugally as possible, we do have certain necessary expenses. These include:

Outreach to the Poor
Utilities
Maintenance and Repairs
Educational Costs (seminary tuition, books, etc.)
Auto, Building, and Health Insurance

Insurance, required of us by the Church and the state, is our single largest expense. God is blessing us with many new vocations; therefore, our financial needs are increasing. And so we humbly make known these growing needs to those who might wish to support us, trusting that each one will freely give what they decide upon in their heart (see 2 Corinthians 9:7), according to their means and the guidance of the Holy Spirit. We are deeply grateful to all of our benefactors and remember them daily in our prayers.

To help with the poor, make checks payable to: St. Francis Center or Padre Pio Shelter (our general charity account). To help the community, please make checks payable to Franciscan Friars of the Renewal.

Offerings may be sent to:

Fr. Benedict Groeschel, C.F.R.
Box 55
Larchmont, NY 10538

Acknowledgements

A book like this does not come about easily. It comes about only with the help of many good people who are willing to drop everything else to work on it — people who share the belief that a publication like this has the potential to help many people of good will.

Special thanks from the acquisitions editor to:

Father Glenn Sudano, C.F.R., the Community Servant of the Franciscan Friars of the Renewal, for taking time out of his very busy schedule to write the Introduction and to facilitate many of the menial tasks that are necessary to bring a book to publication. If you wish to donate to the good work of the Franciscan Friars of the Renewal, please read "How You Can Help the Franciscan Friars of the Renewal" on pages 119-121 of this book.

Joe Campo, who runs St. Francis House (a home for young men founded by Father Benedict in 1967), Youth 2000 NY, and the Grassroots Renewal Project, for the images of Father Benedict that grace the front and back covers of this book. The Grassroots Renewal Project has some terrific evangelization materials available on their website (www.grassroots renewal.com).

David Miller, the webmaster for the Franciscan Friars of the Renewal, for making information pertaining to Father Benedict's recovery available to all of us through their website.

Darrin Malone, for his quick copyediting job.

Monica Haneline, for the quick cover design.

Father Benedict wishes to thank:

Brother Daniel and Brother Peter, Franciscan Friars of the Renewal, who provided their services as full-time practical nurses. Since my release from the hospital, many friars have assisted me under the coordination of *Brother Lawrence*.

My sister *Marjule Groeschel Drury*, who stayed by my side for weeks and coordinated my treatment at the hospital in Orlando.

David Burns and Father John Lynch, who were not only faithful at the time of the accident — which they almost witnessed — but have stuck by me ever since.

The wonderful *staff at Orlando Regional Medical Center* in Orlando, Florida, who literally kept me alive by their dedication and skill.

Volunteers like *John Delgado*, who went to great personal sacrifice to care for the friars and other visitors who came to see me in Florida.

The *staffs at Sound Shore Medical Center and Schaffer Nursing Home* in New Rochelle, New York, and *the staff at Burke Rehabilitation Hospital* in White Plains, New York, who have provided wonderful care for me.

My therapists, *Richard Marx and Paul Loftus*, who have moved me along greatly in my recovery.

The generous *benefactors who have come to the aid* of the friars and assisted with expenses not covered by insurance — they are still continuing to help!

Father Gene Fulton and the staff of Trinity Retreat House, who have responded like family.

And finally, I am ever grateful to *all of the people*, literally tens of thousands of them, who took the time to send me a card or e-mail and who have prayed so fervently for me.